INCLUSIONARY ZONING

A GUIDE TO ORDINANCES AND THE LAW

C. Tyler Mulligan and James L. Joyce

UNC
SCHOOL OF
GOVERNMENT

The School of Government at the University of North Carolina at Chapel Hill works to improve the lives of North Carolinians by engaging in practical scholarship that helps public officials and citizens understand and improve state and local government. Established in 1931 as the Institute of Government, the School provides educational, advisory, and research services for state and local governments. The School of Government is also home to a nationally ranked graduate program in public administration and specialized centers focused on information technology, environmental finance, and civic education for youth.

As the largest university-based local government training, advisory, and research organization in the United States, the School of Government offers up to 200 courses, seminars, and specialized conferences for more than 12,000 public officials each year. In addition, faculty members annually publish approximately fifty books, book chapters, bulletins, and other reference works related to state and local government. Each day that the General Assembly is in session, the School produces the *Daily Bulletin*, which reports on the day's activities for members of the legislature and others who need to follow the course of legislation.

Operating support for the School of Government's programs and activities comes from many sources, including state appropriations, local government membership dues, private contributions, publication sales, course fees, and service contracts. Visit www.sog.unc.edu or call 919.966.5381 for more information on the School's courses, publications, programs, and services.

Michael R. Smith, DEAN
Thomas H. Thornburg, SENIOR ASSOCIATE DEAN
Frayda S. Bluestein, ASSOCIATE DEAN FOR FACULTY DEVELOPMENT
Todd A. Nicolet, ASSOCIATE DEAN FOR OPERATIONS
Ann Cary Simpson, ASSOCIATE DEAN FOR DEVELOPMENT AND COMMUNICATIONS
Bradley G. Volk, ASSOCIATE DEAN FOR ADMINISTRATION

FACULTY

Gregory S. Allison
David N. Ammons
Ann M. Anderson
A. Fleming Bell, II
Maureen M. Berner
Mark F. Botts
Michael Crowell
Shea Riggsbee Denning
James C. Drennan
Richard D. Ducker
Joseph S. Ferrell
Alyson A. Grine
Norma Houston (on leave)
Cheryl Daniels Howell
Jeffrey A. Hughes
Willow S. Jacobson

Robert P. Joyce
Kenneth L. Joyner
Diane M. Juffras
Dona G. Lewandowski
James M. Markham
Janet Mason
Christopher B. McLaughlin
Laurie L. Mesibov
Kara A. Millonzi
Jill D. Moore
Jonathan Q. Morgan
Ricardo S. Morse
C. Tyler Mulligan
David W. Owens
William C. Rivenbark
Dale J. Roenigk

John Rubin
John L. Saxon
Jessica Smith
Karl W. Smith
Carl W. Stenberg III
John B. Stephens
Charles Szypszak
Shannon H. Tufts
Vaughn Upshaw
Aimee N. Wall
Jeffrey B. Welty
Richard B. Whisnant
Gordon P. Whitaker
Eileen R. Youens

Contents

Introduction

To many local government leaders, it is readily apparent that market forces favor the development of high-end housing over affordable housing. Developers, who earn higher profit margins on high-end homes, are motivated to build those homes. Local government leaders, too, may prefer for developers to build higher-priced housing, because under the property tax system, homes carrying higher values also generate greater tax revenues. Partly as a result of these incentive structures, in many communities high-end residential development far outpaces development of affordable housing for low- or moderate-income households.[1]

Local governments throughout the United States have long recognized this affordability gap and have employed a variety of policy tools to increase the supply of affordable housing. In North Carolina, local governments have typically relied on publicly subsidized affordable housing construction programs. In an effort to reduce reliance on public subsidies, a number of local governments are now turning to regulatory approaches that rely upon the private market to increase the supply of affordable housing.[2]

One regulatory approach that has received increased attention in North Carolina and across the country is inclusionary zoning.[3] Inclusionary zoning ordinances encourage participating developers to set aside a percentage of the units they build for housing that is affordable to households in a certain income bracket, and they require developers to maintain the affordability of the set-aside units for a period of time. These set-aside units are called inclusionary or affordable units. The goal of inclusionary zoning is not solely to produce affordable units; inclusionary zoning is undertaken to ensure that new residential developments contain housing with an appropriate mix of affordability that reflects the income ranges of persons living and working in the community.

Public officials, housing advocates, and concerned citizens typically want to know what choices they have in designing inclusionary zoning ordinances for their communities. In answering that question, it is important to point out that an inclusionary zoning ordinance cannot be implemented with a mere one-line council resolution stating that developers must ensure that 20 percent of the units they build are affordable to households with incomes at or below the area median wage. Nor is there one model inclusionary zoning ordinance that can be readily replicated. Rather, each locality faces different circumstances, and the most effective inclusionary zoning ordinance will be tailored to fit the particular community and the housing market it serves. Those seeking to enact an inclusionary zoning ordinance need to be aware of the nuances and complexity involved.

A number of available resources describe various inclusionary zoning policy choices, while others address the legal aspects. However, no one guide addresses all of the issues to help translate policy decisions into a working ordinance. This publication aims to fill that gap. It explains the major policy decisions associated with inclusionary zoning and provides the legal context for those decisions. Examples from existing inclusionary zoning programs illustrate specific choices.[4]

This publication assumes that general land use ordinances are already in place and functioning, and so it does not describe, for example, the components of a general zoning ordinance and its accompanying procedural requirements.[5] Rather, it provides policy makers with a menu of choices and accompanying examples of provisions that can be assembled into an inclusionary zoning ordinance tailored to an individual community.[6] The examples used throughout this publication, however, are intended to be illustrative only, so a policy's inclusion should not be viewed as an endorsement of that policy as a best practice.

Listed below are the localities from which the examples are drawn. Although not every North Carolina locality employing inclusionary zoning is mentioned here, as many as possible are included due to the North Carolina focus of this publication. Featured North Carolina programs include the following:

- Town of Davidson, North Carolina[7]
- Town of Carrboro, North Carolina[8]
- Town of Chapel Hill, North Carolina[9]

- Dare County, North Carolina[10]
- Town of Kill Devil Hills, North Carolina[11]
- Town of Manteo, North Carolina[12]
- City of Winston-Salem/Forsyth County, North Carolina[13]

Inclusionary zoning programs from other U.S. cities and counties were also reviewed for this publication. Programs from the localities listed below have been included for one or more of the following reasons:

- The program exhibits longevity, which increases the likelihood that its provisions have been tested and refined over time.
- The program has produced high numbers of units, which indicates that it has been heavily utilized and its provisions tested by such use.
- The program is frequently referenced in inclusionary zoning literature.
- The program employs a unique or thoughtful approach to an issue raised in this publication.
- The program adds geographic diversity to our list of surveyed programs.

Featured out-of-state programs include the following:

- City of Boulder, Colorado[14]
- City of Burlington, Vermont[15]
- Fairfax County, Virginia[16]
- Montgomery County, Maryland[17]
- City of Napa, California[18]
- City of Sacramento, California[19]
- City of San Diego, California[20]
- City of Santa Fe, New Mexico[21]

It should be noted that none of the ordinances is presented in its entirety, and any specific provision might not prove workable or productive when applied in the context of a different community. The primary consideration in selecting these examples was to illustrate how various localities approach the policy decisions discussed in this publication.

Notes

1. *See* BARBARA J. LIPMAN, CENTER FOR HOUSING POLICY, SOMETHING'S GOTTA GIVE: WORKING FAMILIES AND THE COST OF HOUSING 11–12, (2005), *available at* www.nhc.org/pdf/pub_nc_sgg_04_05.pdf; Douglas R. Porter, *The Promise and Practice*

of Inclusionary Zoning, in GROWTH MANAGEMENT AND AFFORDABLE HOUSING: DO THEY CONFLICT? 213–14 (Anthony Downs ed., 2004).

2. For an overview of local government authority to increase the supply of affordable housing, see ANITA BROWN-GRAHAM, AFFORDABLE HOUSING AND NORTH CAROLINA LOCAL GOVERNMENTS (UNC School of Government 2006).

3. Inclusionary zoning is often just one component of a broader housing program to increase production of affordable housing units. Many different labels have been applied to these programs, such as "affordable," "moderately priced," "inclusionary," "family," "life-cycle," or "workforce" housing programs.

4. Commentary on the legal risks associated with a specific policy choice is provided where possible, but in settling questions of law, there is no substitute for the advice of the city or county attorney.

5. For a comprehensive treatment of land use law, see generally DAVID W. OWENS, LAND USE LAW IN NORTH CAROLINA (UNC School of Government 2006).

6. For an idea of the breadth of variation in existing inclusionary zoning programs, their state regulatory environments, and their successes, see Jenny Schuetz, Rachel Meltzer, and Vicki Been, *31 Flavors of Inclusionary Zoning: Comparing Policies from San Francisco, Washington, DC, and Suburban Boston,* 75 JOURNAL OF THE AMERICAN PLANNING ASSOCIATION 441 (2009).

7. TOWN OF DAVIDSON, N.C., PLANNING ORDINANCE § 6.3 (2009), *available at* www.ci.davidson.nc.us/DocumentView.aspx?DID=1412, and TOWN OF DAVIDSON, N.C., PLANNING ORDINANCE § 23.2 (2009), *available at* www.ci.davidson.nc.us/DocumentView.aspx?DID=1316.

8. CARRBORO, N.C., TOWN CODE ch. 15, art. XII (2009), *available at* www.ci.carrboro.nc.us/PZI/LUO.htm.

9. Town of Chapel Hill, N.C., Ordinance 2010-06-21/O-11 (codified at CODE OF ORDINANCES OF THE TOWN OF CHAPEL HILL, Appendix A (Land Use Management Ordinance) § 3.10 (2010)), *available at* www.ci.chapel-hill.nc.us/index.aspx?page=115. This recently enacted ordinance supersedes an earlier resolution that is also cited in this publication. *See* Town of Chapel Hill, N.C., Resolution 2000-03-06/R-4 (Mar. 6, 2000), *available at* www.townofchapelhill.org/index.aspx?page=579.

10. DARE COUNTY, N.C., CODE OF ORDINANCES tit. XV, ch. 155, app. A (Zoning Ordinance) (2008), *available at* www.amlegal.com/library/nc/dareco.shtml.

11. TOWN OF KILL DEVIL HILLS, N.C., CODE OF ORDINANCES tit. I, ch. 10 and tit. XV, ch. 153 (2008), *available at* www.amlegal.com/library/nc/killdevilhills.shtml.

12. TOWN OF MANTEO, N.C., ZONING CODE art. XI (2009), *available at* www.townofmanteo.com.

13. CITY OF WINSTON-SALEM/FORSYTH COUNTY, N.C., UNIFIED DEVELOPMENT ORDINANCES § 3-9.1–3-9.6 (2008), *available at* www.cityofws.org/Home/Departments/Planning/ZoningAndSubdivision/Articles/UDOAndAmendments.

14. CITY OF BOULDER, COLO., REV. CODE ch. 9-13 (2009), *available at* www.colocode.com/boulderpdf/chapter9-13.pdf.

15. CITY OF BURLINGTON, VT., COMPREHENSIVE DEVELOPMENT ORDINANCE art. 9 (2009), *available at* www.ci.burlington.vt.us/planning/zoning/zn_ordinance/ article_09_housing.pdf.

16. COUNTY OF FAIRFAX, VA., ZONING ORDINANCE art. 2 (2009), *available at* www.fairfaxcounty.gov/dpz/zoningordinance/.

17. MONTGOMERY COUNTY, MD., CODE REGS. (COMCOR) ch. 25A (2003), *available at* www.amlegal.com/library/md/montgomeryco.shtml.

18. CITY OF NAPA, CAL., MUN. CODE ch. 15.94 (1999 & 2005), *available at* http://74.205.120.199/images/cityclerk/MunicipalCode/Title15/Chapters/15.94.pdf. Napa's ordinance was the subject of a significant legal challenge in 2000. *See* Home Builders Ass'n of N. Cal. v. City of Napa, 90 Cal. App. 4th 188, 196–97 (2001).

19. SACRAMENTO, CAL., CITY CODE tit. 17, div. VI, ch. 17.190 (2009), *available at* www.qcode.us/codes/sacramento/.

20. CITY OF SAN DIEGO, CAL., MUN. CODE ch. 14, art. 2, div. 13 (2008), *available at* http://docs.sandiego.gov/municode/MuniCodeChapter14/Ch14Art02Division13.pdf, and CITY OF SAN DIEGO, CAL., INCLUSIONARY AFFORDABLE HOUS. IMPLEMENTATION & MONITORING PROCEDURES MANUAL (revised Mar. 2008), *available at* www.sandiego.gov/development-services/news/pdf/ahprocmanual.pdf.

21. SANTA FE, N.M., CITY CODE ch. XXVI (2009), *available at* http://clerkshq.com/ default.ashx?clientsite=Santafe-nm.

1

Laying the Groundwork:
Collecting Data and Raising Awareness

Prior to drafting an inclusionary zoning ordinance, it is important to determine whether inclusionary zoning is truly the right approach for a particular community. While there are circumstances in which inclusionary zoning can be a valuable tool, other means of providing affordable housing may be better suited for certain communities.

In examining the utility of inclusionary zoning and how a program might be tailored to a community, it is helpful to review the body of existing research analyzing the effects of inclusionary zoning. It is also important to understand the characteristics of communities in which inclusionary zoning tends to be most effective and to commission a housing needs assessment for the community in order to learn about local conditions.

Effects of Inclusionary Zoning

Advocates on both sides of the inclusionary zoning debate frame the discussion by describing the consequences of enacting inclusionary zoning. The debate typically centers on the following questions, each of which will be discussed in turn:

1. Are inclusionary zoning programs effective in producing new affordable housing?
2. How will inclusionary zoning affect the broader housing market in terms of housing starts, housing prices, and the type of housing produced?

Effectiveness

Research to date has shown that even though inclusionary zoning ordinances have been effective in producing affordable housing units,[1] the quantity produced has not been independently sufficient to satisfy the demand for affordable housing in the implementing jurisdictions.[2] Therefore, a community considering inclusionary zoning may also wish to consider other supplemental measures as part of a comprehensive affordable housing strategy.[3]

Research has not yet identified any must-have elements of a productive inclusionary zoning ordinance. One report from New York University's Furman Center for Real Estate and Urban Policy, published in the *Journal of the American Planning Association*, examined inclusionary zoning programs in the San Francisco Bay, Boston, and Washington, DC, metropolitan areas. The authors of the report concluded that although the programs they examined varied greatly, only a few program variables had a statistically significant effect on the number of units the program produced.[4] Specifically, the study found that programs with density bonuses[5] produced more units than those without,[6] and programs with exemptions for smaller developments (that is, those of five to ten units or fewer) likewise produced more units.[7] However, given the relatively small sample size and the limited range of variation within regions (for example, programs in the Boston area tended to be similar to one another, even if they were quite different from programs in the Bay Area), these results should be interpreted with some caution.[8] In the absence of more conclusive studies identifying key elements of an inclusionary zoning program, local policy makers crafting an ordinance are advised to study all of the options and examine them in light of local conditions.[9]

Impacts on the Broader Housing Market

Contemporary research has focused on three effects of inclusionary zoning on broader housing markets: (1) number of housing starts, (2) price of housing, and (3) type of housing produced.

Housing Starts

Examinations of housing starts following implementation of inclusionary zoning appear to quell fears that inclusionary zoning will slow housing production. For instance, a study of California localities published by the National Housing Conference reviewed housing starts from 1981 through 2001 and compared twenty-eight communities—some with inclusionary zoning and some without.[10] This study found that in almost every surveyed city or town, housing starts actually *increased* after the passage of inclusionary zoning ordinances.[11] The study, which employed a land residual analysis,[12] concluded that development projects remained financially feasible following the enactment of inclusionary zoning, and that incentives offered by the communities played a role in that result.[13] A more recent study, undertaken by the National Center for Smart Growth Research and Education at the University of Maryland-College Park,[14] examined California housing markets in 369 municipalities between 1988 and 2005 and found that inclusionary zoning programs had small positive effects on overall housing starts, but the results were not statistically significant.[15] These studies did not find a negative impact on overall housing starts.

Housing Prices

Findings about the price effects of inclusionary zoning have been mixed. A Reason Public Policy Institute study calculated that inclusionary zoning added cost to market-rate homes.[16] However, a more recent study by researchers from the University of Maryland and Boise State University found that although housing prices tended to be roughly 2 percent higher in localities with inclusionary zoning policies,[17] the price increase applied almost entirely to more-expensive housing. The study demonstrated that inclusionary zoning programs resulted in a 5 percent increase in the price of housing that sold for more than $187,000 (in 1988 dollars), but the price of housing below that threshold actually *fell* by 0.8 percent in communities with inclusionary zoning ordinances.[18] Thus, in some cases inclusionary zoning will put upward pressure on home prices, but this effect is more likely to be seen at higher price points where buyers are somewhat less sensitive to price fluctuations.[19]

Type of Housing Produced

Inclusionary zoning appears to have an effect on the type of housing that is built. The aforementioned study by the National Center for Smart Growth Research and Education found that inclusionary zoning ordinances in California tended to result in smaller unit sizes and construction of a higher ratio of multifamily to single-family homes.[20] In communities with inclusionary zoning, this study estimated that, holding other variables constant, the proportion of housing starts made up of single-family homes was seven percentage points lower than in communities without inclusionary zoning.[21]

Additionally, the mean housing size in areas with inclusionary zoning ordinances was roughly 48 square feet smaller than in those without inclusionary zoning.[22] In some cases, the type of inclusionary zoning ordinance seemed to affect the result: the increase in the share of multifamily construction was more pronounced in areas where the minimum development size (that is, the minimum number of housing units) subject to the inclusionary zoning ordinance was lower and where the number of required affordable units was higher.[23]

Prime Conditions for Inclusionary Zoning

The utility of inclusionary zoning will be different for each community, but housing analysts believe that inclusionary zoning is most productive in strong housing markets.[24] Since inclusionary zoning ordinances frequently require that a *percentage* of all new housing units meet certain affordability criteria, greater demand for new development means more affordable units will be built. Greater demand for housing may also make the incentives often used to encourage the provision of affordable units—such as density bonuses or fast-track development approvals—more effective.

Furthermore, inclusionary zoning policies tend to be more successful in areas with ample available, developable (or re-developable) land. Although inclusionary zoning ordinances typically apply to infill areas and can lead to successful infill developments (as long as flexibility measures and housing demand are adequate), some commentators believe that the highest returns from inclusionary zoning will be seen in areas that are not yet built out or approaching build-out.[25]

Conducting a Housing Needs Assessment

The findings discussed above are helpful only when applied in the context of the local housing situation. A key source of information on the local housing market is a housing needs assessment, also sometimes referred to as a linkage study or nexus study.[26] A comprehensive needs assessment not only provides data that will prove invaluable during the policy-making process, but it may also supply an important component of the local government's legal justification for the implementation of an inclusionary program.[27]

Table 1. Undersupply of Housing Units by Income Level

Percent Median Area Income	Units Needed in 2002	Units Needed in 2007
0-30	270	302
31-50	168	247
51-80	113	303
81-100	121	2
Totals	**672**	**854**

To support decisions about inclusionary zoning, the following information can be obtained from existing local development planning documents[28] or requested as part of a needs assessment:[29]

Analysis of current housing supply gaps at various household income levels. This analysis compares the number of local workers earning a certain level of income to the number of housing units available for rent or for purchase at a price considered affordable to that income level. The analysis is performed at several different levels of income and is used to determine which income groups, if any, have housing needs that could be met through an inclusionary zoning policy. An example of such a comparison developed for a North Carolina county is provided in Table 1, above.[30]

Future trends in housing demand and supply. This is similar to the housing supply gap analysis described above, but it analyzes demographic, employment, and market trends to offer a glimpse of potential housing supply gaps in the future.

Linkage between planned residential or commercial development and increased demand for additional affordable housing.[31] The linkage between additional development and an increase in demand for affordable housing is intuitive but difficult to quantify. For example, suppose that new market-rate residential units are priced for sale to higher-income households. Residents of that new residential development will inevitably drive demand for additional commercial services. This heightened demand for services, in turn, requires local service businesses to hire additional workers (many at low wage levels). A linkage study would attempt to quantify the link, if any, between the increase in market-rate housing and the corresponding increase in demand for lower-cost housing for service workers.

Identification of specific geographic areas within the jurisdiction experiencing high housing demand. Because inclusionary zoning policies tend to produce more housing units in areas experiencing rapid growth or high housing demand and those conditions may not exist in every neighborhood or section of a locality, this information may be helpful in determining whether an inclusionary zoning program should be limited to one part of a locality where it is likely to be most effective.

Explanation of existing land use controls and barriers to affordability. Requirements for large lot sizes, extensive setbacks, and low density tend to discourage the production of housing affordable to low- and moderate-income households. For some communities, easing these requirements alone could serve to improve local housing affordability.

An assessment of the profitability of development in the area. Having an idea of the profit margins earned by developers in the community may be helpful in gauging both developers' potential resistance to inclusionary zoning requirements and the extent to which those requirements might affect developers' profitability (if at all).[32]

Notes

1. Jenny Schuetz, Rachel Meltzer, and Vicki Been, *31 Flavors of Inclusionary Zoning: Comparing Policies from San Francisco, Washington, DC, and Suburban Boston*, 75 Journal of the American Planning Association at 452 (2009). ("These data reveal that IZ [inclusionary zoning] programs have produced a significant number of affordable housing units . . . . This was a notable achievement during a time period when federal and state subsidies for affordable housing production were sharply reduced.")

2. *Id.* (finding in its review of programs in the Washington, DC, San Francisco, and Boston metropolitan areas that "there is still considerable need for affordable housing, especially affordable rental housing, in all three regions); *see also* Benjamin Powell and Edward Stringham, Reason Foundation, Housing Supply and Affordability: Do Affordable Housing Mandates Work? 5 (April 2004), *available at* http://reason.org/files/020624933d4c04a615569374fdbeef41.pdf ("For the 5.5-year period over 2001–2006, the Association of Bay Area Governments (ABAG) projected the Bay Area's affordable housing need for very low, low, and moderate income households to be 133,195 units, or 24,217 per year. Over the past 30 years, however, inclusionary zoning throughout the entire Bay Area has produced an average of only 228 units per year.").

3. For a general examination of affordable housing measures employed in North Carolina, see Anita Brown-Graham, Affordable Housing and North Carolina Local Governments (UNC School of Government 2006).

4. Schuetz et al., note 1 above, at 452–53 (describing statistical analysis that found that only the number of years a program was in place, the presence of a density bonus, and the minimum project size had a statistically significant effect on the number of units produced).

5. Density bonuses permit more units to be constructed on a parcel than would otherwise be permitted in the absence of the bonus. For more about density bonuses, what they are, and how they work, see "Density Bonuses" in Chapter 4.

6. Schuetz et al., note 1 above, at 453.

7. *Id.*

8. *Id.* at 452 ("Ideally, we would like to draw conclusions about how the characteristics and structure of IZ [inclusionary zoning] programs affect the amount of affordable housing produced. However, several limitations of the existing data and the nature of IZ programs hinder our ability to do so conclusively.").

9. *Id.* at 454.

10. David Rosen, *Inclusionary Housing and Its Impact on Housing and Land Markets*, *in* 3 NATIONAL HOUSING CONFERENCE AFFORDABLE HOUSING POLICY REVIEW: INCLUSIONARY ZONING: THE CALIFORNIA EXPERIENCE 38, 41 (2004), *available at* www.nhc.org/media/documents/IZ_CA_experiencet.pdf. *See also* DAVID PAUL ROSEN & ASSOCS., CITY OF LOS ANGELES INCLUSIONARY ZONING STUDY ES-1, prepared for the Los Angeles Housing Department (Sept. 25, 2002), *available at* http://lahd.lacity.org/lahdinternet/InclusionaryHousingStudy/tabid/300/Default.aspx (" . . . adoption of an inclusionary housing program is not associated with a negative effect on housing production. In fact, in most jurisdictions . . . housing production increased, sometimes drastically, after passage of inclusionary housing ordinances.").

11. Rosen, note 10 above, at 38. The only exception was Oceanside, a town near San Diego located adjacent to the Camp Pendleton Marine Corps base—its inclusionary zoning ordinance was adopted in 1991, at the same time that the first Gulf War caused vacancy rates in the military community to soar.

12. Rosen, note 10 above, at 42. Land residual analysis involves calculating the value of a piece of land based on its income potential (if developed) minus costs of development and developer profit. If the land value generated by the formula is negative or is less than a seller is willing to accept (based on market comparables), the development is not financially feasible.

13. Rosen, note 10 above, at 42–46. Rosen examined scenarios involving a variety of incentive options, including density bonuses, deferral of development fees, and off-site compliance options.

14. GERRIT-JAN KNAAP, ANTONIO BENTO, AND SCOTT LOWE, NATIONAL CENTER FOR SMART GROWTH RESEARCH AND EDUCATION, HOUSING MARKET IMPACTS OF INCLUSIONARY ZONING (Feb. 2008), *available at* www.smartgrowth.umd.edu/research/pdf/KnaapBentoLowe-InclusionaryHousing.pdf.

15. *See id.* at 10–11 (finding that overall housing starts in municipalities were 0.15 percent greater in municipalities with an inclusionary zoning program compared to those without, but the estimate was not statistically significant at the 90 percent confidence level).

16. POWELL AND STRINGHAM, note 2 above, at 17. The authors of the study claim an average per-unit increase of $45,721, although what percentage of home price this represents is uncertain, particularly since the average *difference* in price between a market-rate

unit and an affordable-housing unit in the communities studied was over $300,000. Powell and Stringham also based their calculations purely on price differentials and did not attempt to estimate the value of incentives.

17. KNAAP ET AL., note 14 above, at 12.

18. *Id.* at 12–13.

19. *Id.* at 1–2.

20. *Id.* at 1.

21. *Id.* at 11 ("Holding all other variables constant, the share of single family housing starts in municipalities that implemented inclusionary zoning programs was nearly seven percentage points lower than those municipalities that did not implement such a program.").

22. *Id.* at 13.

23. KNAAP ET AL., note 14 above, at 11.

24. Douglas R. Porter, *The Promise and Practice of Inclusionary Zoning, in* GROWTH MANAGEMENT AND AFFORDABLE HOUSING: DO THEY CONFLICT? 215, 220 (Anthony Downs ed., 2004). *See also* ENTERPRISE COMMUNITY PARTNERS, INCLUSIONARY ZONING: PROGRAM DESIGN CONSIDERATIONS 2 (2004).

25. *See* KAREN DESTOREL BROWN, THE BROOKINGS INSTITUTION CENTER ON URBAN AND METROPOLITAN POLICY, *Expanding Affordable Housing Through Inclusionary Zoning: Lessons From the Washington Metropolitan Area* 18 (Oct. 2001).

26. The terms "linkage study" and "nexus study" are occasionally used to refer to housing needs assessments because these assessments are developed in order to provide legal justification for an inclusionary zoning policy by connecting the ordinance's regulatory measures to local housing needs. In some cases, a relatively precise determination of the number of affordable housing units required in the community may be helpful. For more on how these studies are connected to the underlying legal issues, see "Takings" in the Legal Appendix.

27. *See* BUSINESS AND PROFESSIONAL PEOPLE FOR THE PUBLIC INTEREST, OPENING THE DOOR TO INCLUSIONARY ZONING 47 (2003) (hereinafter BPI) ("By completing a nexus study, a municipality may avoid a legal challenge to its Inclusionary Housing Ordinance by showing [a connection between the need the ordinance addresses and the ordinance provisions] before any disputes arise. Third, if the ordinance is challenged in court, the municipality can turn to the nexus study as justification for the Inclusionary Housing Program."); see also "Takings" in the Legal Appendix.

28. An example of an existing planning document that may include this data is the locally generated HUD Consolidated Plan. Affordability Mismatch data can be obtained directly from HUD's Comprehensive Housing Affordability Strategy (CHAS) data set, *available at* http://socds.huduser.org/chas/index.html.

29. Examples of housing assessments in North Carolina include CHATHAM COUNTY AFFORDABLE HOUSING TASK FORCE, CHATHAM COUNTY AFFORDABLE HOUSING RECOMMENDATIONS: A REPORT TO THE CHATHAM COUNTY BOARD OF COMMISSIONERS (2009), *available at* www.chathamnc.org/Modules/ShowDocument.aspx?documentid=7926; WILLIAM M. ROHE AND SPENCER COWAN,

WORKFORCE HOUSING NEEDS IN BRUNSWICK COUNTY, NORTH CAROLINA (UNC Center for Urban and Regional Studies 2007) (prepared for the North Carolina Association of Community Development Corporations), *available at* www.bho2020.org/study-Download2.html; and BAY AREA ECONOMICS AND TDA, INC., CITY OF RALEIGH, NORTH CAROLINA HOUSING MARKET ANALYSIS AND HOUSING NEEDS ASSESSMENT (2005) (prepared for City of Raleigh, North Carolina, Community Development Department), *available at* www.docstoc.com/docs/18264165/City-of-Raleigh-North-Carolina-Housing-Market-Analysis-and.

30. CHATHAM COUNTY AFFORDABLE HOUSING TASK FORCE, CHATHAM COUNTY HOUSING NEEDS ASSESSMENT UPDATE 34 (2008) (prepared by The Wooten Company Planning Department), *available at* www.chathamnc.org/Modules/ShowDocument.aspx?documentid=5166.

31. BPI, note 27 above, at 47–50, discusses linkage studies and how to undertake the necessary analysis.

32. As a practical matter, this information may be most usefully displayed by providing a comparison between two versions of a hypothetical *pro forma* income statement (i.e., a spreadsheet or table displaying future projections of income, expenses, developer's fees, and profit for a business operation or development): The first statement would display the income and expense projections for a representative development prior to enactment of an inclusionary zoning policy, and the second statement would display projections as they might appear following enactment of an inclusionary zoning policy, factoring in incentives such as density bonuses, fee waivers, and fast-track permitting. Alternatively, a land residual analysis can be used to estimate financial feasibility of projects before and after an inclusionary zoning ordinance. *See* Rosen, note 10 above, 42–46. For a description of common inclusionary zoning incentives, see Chapter 4.

2

Preamble: Establishing
Legal Authority for the Ordinance

A preamble section conveys the various rationales and sources of author-ity upon which the local government relied in developing an inclusionary zoning ordinance. In the context of inclusionary zoning, preambles are not merely flowery introductions to the law but may actually prove determina-tive in evaluating the legality of the ordinance. Preambles generally include findings that describe the need addressed by the ordinance and a statement of purpose that outlines the purposes for which the ordinance was enacted and the statutory authority on which the ordinance is based. If an inclusion-ary zoning ordinance faces a legal challenge, a reviewing court will look to these statements to evaluate the local government's purpose and authority for enacting the ordinance.[1]

Findings

The governing board's findings explain the factual context in which an inclu-sionary zoning ordinance was enacted. Local governments frequently use the findings section to describe the situation in the community—as understood by the governing board—that prompted the board to act. A findings sec-tion might recite facts drawn from a housing needs assessment,[2] or it may simply explain the governing board's understanding of the situation in the community.

The findings section provides citizens with some insight into the governing board's rationale for enacting an ordinance, but this section may also serve a legal purpose. For instance, if an ordinance is challenged as being arbitrary or unreasonable, a court reviewing the statute may rely upon statements made in the findings section to determine whether or not the governing board did indeed have a rational basis for enacting the ordinance.[3] Legislative findings made in the context of land use regulations are given significant deference by the courts.[4]

EXAMPLES

The following is a sampling of legislative findings that have appeared in inclusionary zoning ordinances from around the country, grouped by the points they address.

Connecting the need for affordable housing to use of scarce remaining land for development:

> The Town finds and determines that additional market rate development would displace and eliminate opportunities for additional affordable housing in the Town unless the restrictions on use established by this Section are included. This displacement would create the following threats to the health, safety, or the general welfare of the community:
> - Increases in travel time and distances for persons who provide services or are employed in the Town, but who cannot find decent, affordable shelter, which in turn increases traffic congestion, reduces air and water quality, and has an adverse impact on public health resulting from excessive commuting; and
> - An imbalance in population diversity . . . .
>
> TOWN OF CHAPEL HILL, N.C., ORDINANCE 2010-06-21/O-11 (codified at CODE OF ORDINANCES OF THE TOWN OF CHAPEL HILL, Appendix A § 3.10 (2010))

> Because remaining land appropriate for residential development within the city is limited, it is essential that a reasonable proportion of such land be developed into housing units affordable to very low-, low- and moderate-income residents and working people. This is particularly true because of the tendency, in the absence of intervention, for large expensive housing to be developed within the city which both reduces opportunities for more affordable housing and contributes to a general rise in prices for all of the housing in the community, thus exacerbating the scarcity of affordable housing within the city.
>
> CITY OF BOULDER, COLO., REV. CODE § 9-13-1(e) (2009)

> Since the remaining land appropriate for new residential development within the town is limited, it is essential that a reasonable proportion of such land be developed into housing units affordable to low and moderate income households and working families.
>
> TOWN OF MANTEO, N.C., ZONING CODE § 11-1 (2009)

A current shortage of affordable housing:

> WHEREAS, The Town of Chapel Hill commissioned a study to calculate the need for affordable housing in Chapel Hill generated by new residential construction, entitled "Calculating the Need for Affordable Housing in Chapel Hill Generated by New Residential Construction" dated April 30, 2009, which documents the need for affordable housing generated by such construction;
>
> TOWN OF CHAPEL HILL, N.C., ORDINANCE 2010-06-21/O-11, SECTION 1 (2010))

> The City is experiencing an increasing shortage of housing affordable to very low and low income households.
>
> CITY OF SACRAMENTO, CAL., ORD. 2000-039 § 1

> Santa Fe is facing a growing shortage of housing that is affordable to a wide range of our population affecting the ability of new graduates, senior citizens, families with children, and employees in industries and services that are vital to a healthy economy to remain living in the city . . .
>
> SANTA FE, N.M., CITY CODE § 26-1.4(E) (2009)

Current development not adequately producing affordable units:

> New residential development does not provide housing opportunities for very low and low income households due to the high cost of newly constructed housing in the City. As a result, low and very low income families are de facto excluded from many new neighborhoods,

creating economic stratification in the City detrimental to the public
health, safety and welfare.

CITY OF SACRAMENTO, CAL., ORD. 2000-039 § 1

New residential development has not provided sufficient housing
opportunities for households with incomes below the area median
income;

SANTA FE, N.M., CITY CODE § 26-1.4(B) (2009)

Promotion of a diverse housing stock:

A diverse housing stock is necessary in this community in order to
serve people of all income levels. Based upon the review and consideration of recent housing studies, reports and analysis, it has become
clear that the provisions of this chapter are necessary in order to preserve some diversity of housing opportunities for the city's residents
and working people.

CITY OF BOULDER, COLO., REV. CODE § 9-13-1(a) (2009)

The diversity of the town's housing stock has declined because of
increasing property values and construction costs. The town recognizes the need to provide affordable housing to low and moderate-
income households in order to maintain a diverse population and to
provide housing for those who live or work in the town.

TOWN OF MANTEO, N.C., ZONING CODE § 11-1 (2009)

The desire to place workers closer to employment and maintain an adequate local workforce:

The program defined by this chapter . . . is necessary to help maintain
a diverse housing stock and to allow working people to have better
access to jobs and upgrade their economic status.

CITY OF BOULDER, COLO., REV. CODE § 9-13-1(b) (2009)

> Without intervention, the trend toward increasing housing prices will result in an inadequate supply of affordable housing for town residents and local employees, which will have a negative impact upon the ability of local employers to maintain an adequate local work force and will otherwise be detrimental to the public health, safety, and welfare of the town and its residents.
>
> TOWN OF MANTEO, N.C., ZONING CODE § 11-1 (2009)

Furthering economic integration:

> The program defined by this chapter . . . is necessary in order to decrease social conflict by lessening the degree of separateness and inequality . . . The regional trend toward increasing housing prices will, without intervention, result in inadequate supplies of affordable housing here for very low-, low- and moderate-income and working people. This in turn will have a negative effect upon the ability of local employers to maintain an adequate local work force.
>
> CITY OF BOULDER, COLO., REV. CODE § 9-13-1(b) (2009)

> Economic diversity fosters social and environmental conditions that protect and enhance the social fabric of the City and are beneficial to the health, safety and welfare of its residents.
>
> CITY OF SACRAMENTO, CAL., ORD. 2000-039 § 1

Statement of Purpose

The statement of purpose connects the governing board's action—namely, enacting an ordinance—to the need outlined in the findings section. For this reason, many preambles blend the statement of purpose with the findings.

Additionally, the statement of purpose presents an opportunity for a governing board to invoke the legal authority upon which it is relying. This serves a particular legal purpose in North Carolina, where local governments possess no inherent regulatory authority to act. Under the state constitution, local governments in North Carolina may not enact regulations unless they have been granted authority to do so by the North Carolina General Assembly.[5] In the case of inclusionary zoning, the General Assembly has not expressly granted authority to local governments to enact inclusionary zoning ordinances, but some have argued that such power can be fairly implied from existing local government authority, such as the zoning,[6] subdivision,[7] housing authority,[8] and police power[9] grants of authority.[10] Some North Carolina local governments have obtained special authority from the General Assembly to enact ordinances resembling inclusionary zoning, and the preamble would be an appropriate place to make reference to such special authority. The assistance of a local government attorney may be necessary to clarify the authority on which an inclusionary zoning ordinance is based.[11]

EXAMPLES

Manteo's ordinance makes no reference to statutory authority but rather declares a general purpose to regulate conditions detrimental to "the public health, safety, and welfare":

> The purpose of this chapter is to promote the public health, safety, and welfare by promoting housing of high quality located in neighborhoods throughout the community for households of all income levels, ages and sizes in order to meet the town's goal of preserving and promoting a culturally and economically diverse population in our community.
>
> TOWN OF MANTEO, N.C., ZONING CODE § 11-1 (2009)

Chapel Hill's recently enacted ordinance makes clear reference to the statutes on which it claims to base its authority:

> WHEREAS, the Town has express authority to establish regulations that protect that health, safety, or welfare of its citizens and the peace and dignity of the city (N.C.G.S. § 160A-174); and
>
> WHEREAS, the Town has express authority to adopt land use plans and to develop ordinances and procedures to implement those plans (N.C.G.S. § 160A-361); and
>
> WHEREAS, the Town's authority under Chapter 160A is broadly construed (N.C.G.S. § 160A-4); and
>
> . . .

WHEREAS, the Town is expressly authorized to enact subdivision and zoning regulations that promote the public health, safety, and the general welfare (N.C.G.S. §§ 160A-372, 160A-381, 160A-383); and

WHEREAS, the Town is expressly authorized to enact zoning regulations that implement the goals and objectives of its comprehensive plan (N.C.G.S. § 160A-383) . . .

TOWN OF CHAPEL HILL, N.C., ORDINANCE 2010-06-21/O-11, SECTION 1 (2010)

Below are examples of purpose statements from other communities around the country.

(b) To ensure the provision of housing that meets the needs of all economic groups by precluding construction of only market rate housing on the limited supply of available land within the City;

(c) To improve the quality of life for all residents by having an economically integrated housing supply throughout the City; and,

(d) To prevent overcrowding and deterioration of the limited supply of affordable housing, and thereby promote the public health, safety and general welfare.

CITY OF BURLINGTON, VT., COMPREHENSIVE DEVELOPMENT ORDINANCE § 9.1.1 (2009)

Purpose. The purpose of this chapter is to establish . . . an inclusionary requirement or an in-lieu fee on developers of residential development projects to mitigate the impacts caused by these development projects on the additional demand for more affordable housing and rising land prices for limited supply of available residential land . . .

CITY OF NAPA, CAL., MUN. CODE § 15.94.010 (1999)

Purpose of Inclusionary Affordable Housing Regulations
The purpose of this Division is to encourage diverse and balanced neighborhoods with housing available for households of all income levels. The intent is to ensure that when developing the limited supply of developable land, housing opportunities for persons of all income levels are provided.

CITY OF SAN DIEGO, CAL., MUN. CODE § 142.1301 (2008)

The purpose of the Santa Fe Homes Program is to:

A. Increase the supply of affordable housing within the Santa Fe area for residents and businesses.

B. Encourage the construction of affordable housing in all areas of the city in accordance with the general plan.

C. Strengthen the unique heterogeneous character of the Santa Fe area by providing a full range of housing choices for all ages, incomes and family sizes.

D. Ensure that residents and future generations can afford to reside within the Santa Fe area.

E. Ensure that affordable housing opportunities are available for those who work and wish to live in the Santa Fe area.

F. Encourage the maintenance of the long term affordability of housing units within the Santa Fe area.

G. Provide affordable housing wherever city utilities are extended beyond the city limits.

H. Foster economic integration by encouraging the availability of a range of housing opportunities in new developments in the Santa Fe area.

I. To provide the benefit of home equity to homeowners of affordable housing similar to those in market rate housing for such purposes as college education and retirement needs and in turn encouraging pride in ownership and maintenance of the affordable housing unit by allowing access to that home equity.

SANTA FE, N.M., CITY CODE § 26-1.3 (2009)

The purposes of this Section are to:

(a) Implement the housing goals of the Boulder Valley Comprehensive Plan;

(b) Promote the construction of housing that is affordable to the community's workforce;

(c) Retain opportunities for people that work in the city to also live in the city;

(d) Maintain a balanced community that provides housing for people of all income levels; and

(e) Insure that housing options continue to be available for very low-income, low-income, and moderate-income residents, for special needs populations and for a significant proportion of those who both work and wish to live in the city.

CITY OF BOULDER, COLO., REV. CODE § 9-13-2 (2009)

Notes

1. The applicable legal tests are described in the Legal Appendix.

2. For example, the Purpose Statement of the Town of Chapel Hill's recently enacted inclusionary zoning ordinance includes a findings section that begins, "Based upon the review and consideration of reports and analyses of the housing supply in the Town . . . ." Town of Chapel Hill, Ordinance 2010-06-21/O-11 (codified at CODE OF ORDINANCES OF THE TOWN OF CHAPEL HILL, Appendix A § 3.10 (2010)).

3. Indeed, inclusionary zoning proponents recommend that a findings section be included in inclusionary zoning ordinances for this very purpose. *See* BUSINESS AND PROFESSIONAL PEOPLE FOR THE PUBLIC INTEREST, OPENING THE DOOR TO INCLU-SIONARY ZONING 47 (2003) (hereinafter BPI); Deborah Collins and Michael Rawson, *Avoiding Constitutional Challenges to Inclusionary Zoning, in* 3 NATIONAL HOUSING CONFERENCE AFFORDABLE HOUSING POLICY REVIEW: INCLUSIONARY ZONING: THE CALIFORNIA EXPERIENCE 32, 32–33 (2004), *available at* www.nhc.org/media/documents/IZ_CA_experiencet.pdf.

4. Berman v. Parker, 348 U.S. 26, 32–33 (1954) (holding that it was a proper exercise of city's police power to condemn private property pursuant to the city's slum clearance program and finding no due process violation, noting, "Subject to specific constitutional limitations, when the legislature has spoken, the public interest has been declared in terms well-nigh conclusive," and, "The concept of the public welfare is broad and inclusive. The values it represents are spiritual as well as physical, aesthetic as well as monetary. It is within the power of the legislature to determine that the community should be beautiful as well as healthy, spacious as well as clean, well-balanced as well as carefully patrolled."). North Carolina courts exercise a similar degree of deference. *See* Zopfi v. City of Wilmington, 273 N.C. 430, 437, 160 S.E.2d 325, 332 (1968) (courts "are not free to substitute their opinion for that of the legislative body so long as there is some plausible basis for the conclusion reached by that body"); *see also In re* Parker, 214 N.C. 51, 55, 197 S.E. 706, 709 (1938) ("[T]he settled rule seems to be that the court will not substitute its judgment for that of the legislative body charged with the primary duty and responsibility of determining whether its action is in the interest of the public health, safety, morals, or general welfare.").

5. N.C. CONST. art. VII, § 1 ("The General Assembly . . . may give such powers and duties to counties, cities and towns, and other governmental subdivisions as it may deem advisable.")

6. N.C. GEN. STAT. (hereinafter G.S.) § 153A-340 (counties), 160A-381 (cities and towns).

7. G.S. 153A-331 (counties), 160A-372 (cities and towns).

8. G.S. Ch. 157 (housing authorities), G.S. 153A-376 (counties), and G.S. 160-456 (cities).

9. G.S. 153A-140 (counties), 160A-174 (cities and towns).

10. For more on how the authority to engage in inclusionary zoning might be implied from existing grants of authority in North Carolina and the risks of relying on such

implied authority, see "Local Government Authority to Enact Inclusionary Zoning in North Carolina" in the Legal Appendix.

11. For a discussion of the concerns surrounding local government authority in North Carolina, see "Local Government Authority to Enact Inclusionary Zoning in North Carolina" in the Legal Appendix.

3

Production Provisions

The engine of an affordable housing ordinance consists of its production provisions, which control the type and quantity of affordable housing to be produced. Production provisions include the level of compulsion (that is, whether the program is mandatory, voluntary, or triggered when an application is made for rezoning); the types and sizes of developments subject to the ordinance; the percentage of affordable housing units to be produced; and the price of units produced under the program.

These provisions are best considered together, because they are interrelated. On the one hand, for example, it may be possible for a development to profitably incorporate a higher percentage of affordable units if those units can be sold or rented at a price that is close to the going market rate for those units.[1] On the other hand, if a development offers housing units that are deeply discounted in order to make them affordable to very low-income households, it may be difficult for that development to accommodate a large number of such units and still remain economically feasible.

Level of Compulsion

The level of compulsion dictates whether participation by developers in the inclusionary zoning program will be mandatory for all new developments of a certain size, required only as a condition for approval of a rezoning request, or entirely voluntary.

In North Carolina, this particular decision carries profound legal implications; therefore, it is necessary to consult with a local government attorney prior to selecting an approach. The legal authority will be different depending on the approach selected. Examples of each of these approaches are found in North Carolina.[2]

Mandatory

Mandatory programs require all new residential developments of a certain size to include some number of affordable units. The affordable units produced under a mandatory program often remain in private hands, but they may be managed by a local government or designated nonprofit.[3]

Mandatory programs are preferred by some because they can be applied to the broadest number of developments and because they produce a predictable quantity of affordable units that remains in step with the overall growth of the community.[4] Opponents claim, however, that a mandatory program unfairly compels developers and buyers of new homes to shoulder the cost of providing affordable housing in the community.[5] Consequently, many mandatory programs provide incentives to developers in order to mitigate some of the perceived negative effects of mandatory compliance.[6]

There are two general legal concerns associated with implementing a mandatory inclusionary zoning program, neither of which presents an absolute barrier, but both of which will likely be raised in debate. First, a mandatory program may be viewed by some as effecting a taking of property for which the owner must be compensated. As a matter of law, however, such a finding in court is highly unlikely unless a developer is required to surrender ownership of affordable units produced.[7] Second, an inclusionary zoning program, if challenged in court, will almost certainly be subjected to a legal test for reasonableness.[8] Mandatory programs can overcome a reasonableness challenge through careful design: this may include addressing an affordable housing need that was documented in a housing needs assessment, as discussed in Chapter 1; offering incentives, which are discussed in Chapter 4; or applying relief mechanisms in the event of hardship, as explained in Chapter 5.

In North Carolina, authority to implement a mandatory inclusionary zoning program is not settled law, but such authority can reasonably be implied from existing zoning, subdivision, housing, and police powers.[9] The basic argument is that local governments possess authority to use zoning to regulate the use of land in the community, and that enacting use regulations governing the mix of affordability in residential developments on scarce developable land is necessarily included within that authority. However, because no explicit authority to enact a mandatory inclusionary zoning program has been granted by the General Assembly, the possibility remains that courts could interpret local government zoning powers narrowly in a way that limits aspects of mandatory inclusionary zoning.[10] With the legal landscape changing frequently, North Carolina local governments seeking to enact mandatory programs will find it necessary to consult closely with a land use or local government attorney. This concern can be eliminated, of course, by obtaining special authority from the North Carolina General Assembly to implement a mandatory program. To date, however, local governments in North Carolina have not succeeded in obtaining such authority.[11]

EXAMPLE

In its simplest form, a mandatory program simply requires that a certain number or percentage of affordable housing units be built in any market-rate development that is subject to the inclusionary requirement.

> *General Requirement.* Except as otherwise provided, 12.5% of the total number of residential units within any development *shall be affordable housing units* and shall be located on the site of the development.
>
> TOWN OF DAVIDSON, N.C., PLANNING ORDINANCE § 6.3.2.B.1 (2008) (emphasis added)

Voluntary

In a voluntary inclusionary zoning program, a developer may proceed with by-right residential development under general zoning policies with no obligation to provide affordable housing, or the developer may opt in to the inclusionary zoning program. This may be done either by applying for a conditional use permit that offers incentives to the developer for producing some minimum number of affordable units or by entering into an agreement with the local government for the provision of inclusionary units.

A common incentive offered to developers for voluntarily constructing affordable housing is a density bonus, which permits the developer to construct more units than would otherwise be permitted in a by-right development. Another form of incentive is the relaxation of strict development controls, such as setback or environmental requirements. Voluntary programs rely heavily upon offering generous incentives to developers to encourage participation. Incentives are discussed in Chapter 4.

Because they do not compel developers to construct affordable units, voluntary programs are the least likely to be challenged in court and the most palatable to potential opponents of inclusionary zoning when initially enacted. However, some communities have seen little production from voluntary programs. For instance, a 2001 survey of municipalities in North Carolina's Research Triangle area found that no affordable housing had been produced as a result of voluntary programs that had been in place for an average of seven years.[12] On the other hand, however, recently enacted North Carolina programs—one in Dare County and the other in Kill Devil Hills—reportedly produced more than two dozen units in a two-year period.

As mentioned above, voluntary programs can be implemented through conditional use permitting. In North Carolina, local governments are authorized to employ conditional use permits as part of a zoning program.[13] The regulations governing such conditional use permits must provide adequate guiding standards for boards charged with reviewing permit applications.[14]

EXAMPLES

A voluntary inclusionary zoning program in Dare County designates a conditional family housing use within any zoning category. Within the family housing use category—provided that certain housing units are priced to be affordable for qualifying households at the median income—the development is eligible for a generous density bonus and relaxation of setback and other requirements. The conditional use permitting process is applied to ensure that the development incorporates the affordable housing units required under the conditional use.

Intent—These standards are intended for use by the private sector in the construction of residential structures for targeted sectors of the year-round population of unincorporated Dare County to address the need for residential housing for this population. *This section establishes eligibility standards and definitions that shall be applied to all private sector developments that propose construction of structures based on these incentives outlined in the following subsections.* These standards shall not be used to authorize private sector developments that are

> marketed for year-round residents or others who do not meet the
> eligibility definitions set forth in subsection (b) of this section.
>   Except as otherwise specifically provided for in this section, *this
> section shall apply as a conditional use in all areas of unincorporated Dare
> County.* All projects authorized under this section shall be subject to
> review as a conditional use permit pursuant to Section 22-68.
>
> DARE COUNTY, N.C., ZONING ORDINANCE § 22-58.3(a) (2008) (emphasis
> added)

In the Winston-Salem/Forsyth County combined planning area,
developers can opt in to the inclusionary program by entering into a
development contract with the local housing department to ensure
compliance.

> 3-9.1 DENSITY INCREASE PERMITTED
>   An increase in the density otherwise permitted in the zoning
> district may be permitted for developments which provide on-site or
> off-site housing opportunities for low- or moderate-income house-
> holds. A contract shall be approved by the County Attorney or City
> Attorney and the Forsyth County Department of Housing (FCDH) or
> the Winston-Salem Housing and Neighborhood Development Depart-
> ment (HND) as a condition of special use district zoning, preliminary
> subdivision approval, or other site plan review guaranteeing that the
> reserved units will be purchased by or rented to qualifying house-
> holds, and shall be binding for a period of not less than fifteen (15)
> years from the date on which the unit is first occupied. The reserved
> lots or rental units shall be indicated on the site plan submitted.
>
> CITY OF WINSTON-SALEM/FORSYTH COUNTY, N.C., UNIFIED DEVELOPMENT ORDINANCES
> § 3-9.1

Conditional

Rather than applying inclusionary requirements to all developments of a
certain size or type within the community, conditional programs impose
requirements only on developments that apply for conditional rezoning. The
affordable set-aside requirement may come in the form of an "expectation"—
the expectation being that applicants for conditional zoning changes will
incorporate plans for affordable housing in their development proposals.

The success of a conditional program will depend largely upon the demand for rezoning. In a community in which growth is strictly controlled—where, for example, little or no land is made available for new residential development under existing zoning—more rezonings might be sought, resulting in a more productive program.

In North Carolina, a conditional program alleviates some of the legal concerns associated with mandatory programs, because local governments possess clear authority to establish conditional zoning schemes.[15] However, under North Carolina law, any conditions or site-specific standards imposed must address the impacts reasonably expected to be generated by the development.[16] There are several ways to show how inclusionary requirements address impacts generated by the development. For example, reference can be made to a housing needs assessment that identifies an undersupply of affordable housing in the community and perhaps articulates how further market-rate development would exacerbate that undersupply.[17] Additionally, in light of a demonstrated need for affordable housing, a local government could express its desire to ensure that any further development of scarce available land incorporates a sufficient supply of affordable housing, or at least a proportional mix of housing consistent with the identified need.[18]

In any event, the design of a conditional zoning scheme requires careful attention to legal requirements, so the outlines of a conditional inclusionary zoning program should be drawn in close consultation with a local government or land use attorney.

EXAMPLE

The language in a 2000 resolution passed by the Town of Chapel Hill implemented a conditional program by establishing an expectation for all rezoning applications.

A RESOLUTION STATING THE COUNCIL'S EXPECTATIONS FOR AFFORDABLE HOUSING AS A COMPONENT OF NEW RESIDENTIAL DEVELOPMENT PROPOSALS

WHEREAS, Chapel Hill's Comprehensive Plan contains the following language: "The Town shall encourage developers of residential developments of 5 or more units to (a) provide 15 percent of their units at prices affordable to low and moderate income households, (b) contribute in-lieu-fees, or (c) propose alternative measures so that the equivalent of 15 percent of their units will be available and affordable to low and moderate income households;" and

WHEREAS, development proposals regularly come before the Town Council seeking approval, but without an affordable housing component;

NOW, THEREFORE, BE IT RESOLVED by the Council of the Town of Chapel Hill that *it is the expectation of the Council that applicants seeking approval of rezoning applications containing a residential component will incorporate a "15 percent affordable" feature into their plans*, and that mechanisms will be proposed to assure ongoing affordability of these so-designated dwelling units.

TOWN OF CHAPEL HILL, N.C., RESOLUTION 2000-03-06/R-4 (Mar. 6, 2000) (emphasis added)

Types of Developments Subject to the Ordinance

An inclusionary zoning ordinance must specify which developments are subject to the operative affordability requirements. Four factors are typically considered:

1. Threshold number of total housing units in the development (for example, five or more units)
2. Use categories (for example, single-family residential, multifamily residential, commercial, or mixed-use commercial and residential)
3. Stage of development (for example, new construction or renovation)
4. Change in tenancy (for example, owner-occupied or rental/tenant-occupied)[19]

Each of these is discussed below.

Threshold Number of Units

Each inclusionary zoning ordinance will have a threshold number of units in a development that triggers the inclusionary requirement or incentive. This threshold may be as few as one or as many as fifty (or more) units, but the threshold should be determined in the context of what is appropriate for the community. If the threshold is set too low, small developments might have difficulty complying with a set-aside percentage or might be forced to resort to a relief mechanism.[20] If it is set too high, developers may avoid the inclusionary requirements by planning and building fewer units in each development. As one observer noted, "A mandate applicable to all developments of 20 or more units commonly results in developments of 19 or fewer units."[21] Some communities attempt to address the latter problem by counting all units created by a developer during any twelve-month period.[22]

EXAMPLES

Manteo applies its minimum threshold both to residential units in a new development and to lots resulting from a subdivision of land.

> The provisions of this chapter shall apply to all new developments that result in or contain five or more residential dwelling units or a new subdivision of land that results in five or more residential lots.
>
> TOWN OF MANTEO, N.C., ZONING CODE § 11-2 (2009)

Fairfax County includes a special provision to keep developers from building large-scale projects in phases so as to avoid the requirements of the ordinance.

> An owner and/or applicant shall not avoid the requirements of this Part by submitting piecemeal applications for rezoning or special exception or piecemeal site plan or subdivision plat submissions for less than fifty (50) dwelling units at any one time. However, an owner and/or applicant may submit a site plan or subdivision plat for less than fifty (50) dwelling units if the owner and/or applicant agrees in

writing that the next application or submission for the site or portion thereof shall meet the requirements of this Part when the total number of dwelling units has reached fifty (50) or more. This written statement shall be recorded among the Fairfax County land records and shall be indexed in the names of all owners of the site or portion thereof . . . .

COUNTY OF FAIRFAX, VA., ZONING ORDINANCE § 2-802(3) (2009)

Burlington's inclusionary zoning ordinance illustrates three points:

1. It applies different size thresholds to different development types.
2. It applies its inclusionary requirements to the aggregate of all developments proposed by a developer during any twelve-month period, to prevent developers from skirting the ordinance by breaking up large projects into a number of smaller developments that individually do not exceed the threshold.
3. It includes a voluntary opt-in provision for small developments seeking to qualify under the ordinance that otherwise would not be required to comply with inclusionary set-asides.

This ordinance provision applies to all subdivisions and planned unit development[s] (PUD) . . . . Any development of five or more residential units in a single structure shall be considered "minor" planned unit developments and shall be subject to the standards of this article. Multiple developments or projects by the same applicant or responsible party within any consecutive twelve (12) month period that in the aggregate equal or exceed the above criteria shall be subject to these regulations.

Except as otherwise provided in this ordinance, these regulations shall apply in the instances specified below.

(a) The creation of five (5) or more residential units through new construction and/or substantial rehabilitation of existing structures, including the development of housing units utilizing development provisions other than those specified in [the following subsection].

(b) Where units are created using the Adaptive Reuse or Residential Conversion criteria [which are described in a different article of the ordinance], this article shall be applicable when at least ten (10) or more dwelling units are created.

(c) An applicant may elect to be subject to the provisions of this article if new units are added to existing units for a total of 5 or more units.

CITY OF BURLINGTON, VT., COMPREHENSIVE DEVELOPMENT ORDINANCE § 9.1.5 (2009)

Use Categories

Inclusionary zoning is usually applied to several different residential use categories, such as single-family, multifamily, or mixed-use with a residential component. However, not all inclusionary zoning programs are applied solely to residential uses. Relying on linkage studies demonstrating that commercial development results in quantifiable demand for affordable housing, some communities have gone further by applying inclusionary zoning to *nonresidential* development. Napa, for example, charges a fee for commercial development on the basis that workers in the jobs located at the development will generate additional demand for affordable housing.[23] Ordinance framers, armed with well-researched housing needs assessments, may wish to consider the nexus between different types of development and affordable housing.[24]

Stage of Development

Stage of development refers to the point in a development project's life at which an inclusionary zoning ordinance applies. Some ordinances apply only at the time of subdivision, and are therefore primarily applicable to new construction. Others regulate infill development and rehabilitation of existing housing by setting a threshold level of renovation (often a change in the number of units) that triggers the inclusionary requirement. Built-out communities can therefore still employ inclusionary zoning policies by, for example, requiring provision of affordable units when major renovations lead to a change in use.[25]

EXAMPLES

Manteo's provision illustrates the application of several use categories and stages of development.

The types of development subject to the provisions of this ordinance include, without limitation, the following:

(1) A development that is new residential construction or new mixed-use construction with a residential component.

(2) A development that is the renovation or reconstruction of an existing multiple family residential structure that increases the number of residential units from the number of units in the original structure by five or more units.

(3) A development that will change the use of an existing building from non-residential to residential having five or more units.

. . .

(5) A new subdivision of land into five or more residential lots.

TOWN OF MANTEO, N.C., ZONING CODE § 11-2 (2009)

Davidson incorporates several unconventional development categories in its broad definition of "development."

The carrying out of any building activity, the making of any material change in the use or appearance of any structure or land, or the subdividing of land into two or more parcels.

A. Except as provided in subsection C hereof, for the purposes of these regulations the following activities or uses shall be considered development:

1. The reconstruction, alteration of the size, or material change in the external appearance of a structure on land or water;

2. A change in the intensity of use of land, such as an increase in the number of dwelling units in a structure or on land or a material increase in the number of businesses, manufacturing establishments, offices, or dwelling units in a structure or on land;

3. Alteration of the shore or bank of a pond, lake, river, or other waterway,

4. Commencement of drilling (except to obtain soil samples), mining, or excavation on a parcel of land;

5. Clearing of land, including clearing or removal of vegetation and including any significant disturbance of vegetation or soil manipulation; or

6. Deposit of refuse, solid or liquid waste, or fill on a parcel of land.

B. Development includes all other activity customarily associated with it. When appropriate to the context development refers to the act of developing or to the result of development. Reference to any specific operation is not intended to mean that the operation or activity when part of other operations or activities is not development. Reference to particular operations is not intended to limit the generality of this definition.

C. For the purposes of these regulations the following operations or uses shall not be considered development; some may, however, require a building permit:

1. Work involving the maintenance, renewal, improvement, or alteration of any structure, if the work affects only the color or decoration of the exterior of the structure or interior alterations that do not change the use for which the structure was constructed.

2. Work involving the maintenance or replacement of existing landscaped areas and existing rights-of-way;

3. A change in use of land or structure from a use within a specified category of use to another use in the same category;

4. A change in the ownership or form of ownership of any parcel or structure;

5. The creation or termination of rights of access, riparian rights, easements, covenants concerning development of land, or other rights in land unless otherwise specifically required by law, or

6. The clearing of survey cuts or other paths of less than four feet in width.

7. Construction of an individual single family home or duplex on a lot that a) is included in an approved master plan or minor subdivision, or b) existed prior to the effective date of this ordinance by a process that did not require subdivisions approval.

TOWN OF DAVIDSON, N.C., PLANNING ORDINANCE § 23.2 (2009)

Change in Tenancy

Some inclusionary zoning ordinances make changes in tenancy, or manner of ownership, subject to inclusionary requirements. This typically occurs when rental units are converted to for-sale or condominium units.[26]

Although it is not uncommon in other states, this practice is likely to be vulnerable if challenged in a North Carolina court. The issue has not been addressed in the context of inclusionary zoning, but North Carolina courts have rejected attempts by local governments to regulate manner of ownership (such as preventing an owner from converting rental units to condominiums).[27] It is therefore likely that a court would view a requirement for affordable units to be created at the time of a condominium conversion as an impermissible regulation of manner of ownership.

Set-Aside Percentage of Affordable Units

Most inclusionary zoning programs require developers to set aside 10 to 30 percent of the total units in a covered development as affordable housing units.[28] In selecting a percentage, the characteristics of the community and the nature of development in the community are important considerations, as are the level of compulsion and the level of affordability required by the ordinance. A housing needs assessment that includes projections of future development may provide some indication of the appropriate percentage to set. While some communities opt for a single, fixed set-aside percentage applicable to all developments, others use tiered or variable percentages.

Fixed Percentage

This common approach applies a single set-aside percentage to all covered developments. The established percentage remains unchanged until the local government's legislative body enacts an adjustment (if ever).

EXAMPLE

Davidson employs a single fixed percentage in its inclusionary zoning ordinance.

> 1. **General Requirement.** Except as otherwise provided, 12.5% of the total number of residential units within any development shall be affordable housing units and shall be located on the site of the development.
> 2. **Calculation.** To calculate the number of affordable housing units, the total number of proposed units, including the affordable units, shall be multiplied by 12.5%. If the product contains a fraction, a fraction of .5 or more shall be rounded up, and a fraction of less than .5 shall be rounded down . . .
>
> TOWN OF DAVIDSON, N.C., PLANNING ORDINANCE § 6.3.2.C (2009)

Tiered or Variable Percentages

Other ordinances establish multiple fixed percentages, where the appropriate percentage applied to a particular development is determined by the characteristics of the development. Examples of tiered set-aside percentages include:

- *Tiering by income.* For example, 5 percent of units must be affordable to households earning 50 percent of Area Median Income (AMI), and 10 percent must be affordable to households earning 80 percent AMI.
- *Variable by affordability of units produced.* For example, if the developer agrees to make its set-aside units affordable to households earning less than 50 percent AMI, then only 5 percent of its units must be affordable; otherwise, the developer must make 15 percent of its units affordable to households earning less than 80 percent AMI.
- *Tiering by the cost of market-rate units.* For example, if the average price of all market-rate units is lower than the community's median price, then only 5 percent of the units must be affordable to households earning less than 80 percent AMI; otherwise, 15 percent of the units must be affordable to households earning less than 80 percent AMI.

Tiered and variable set-asides permit a local government to tailor an ordinance to provide incentives for developers to meet the community's greatest housing needs. Properly designed tiering may place an inclusionary zoning policy on firmer legal footing, because such tailored set-aside requirements will (in theory) be more closely related to the community's demonstrated housing needs at different income levels.[29]

EXAMPLES

Burlington bases the affordable set-aside percentage on the value of the market-rate units in the development.[30]

> For covered projects in which units are offered for rent or sale, a base of fifteen percent (15%) of all of the dwelling units in the project, graduated as specified in Table 9.1.9-1 [below], shall be designated as inclusionary units[.]
>
> This includes any covered project where units are offered for sale via the conveyance of a deed or share for individual units, including fee simple ownership, condominium ownership and cooperative ownership.
>
> **Table 9.1.9-1 Inclusionary Zoning Percentages**
>
> | If the average sale and rental price of project units is affordable to a household earning: | The percentage of units which are subject to rent and sales prices as per Sec. 9.1.10 and are subject to marketing and continued affordability provisions (Sec. 9.1.11 and Sec. 9.1.12) shall be: |
> | --- | --- |
> | Less than 139% of median income | 15% |
> | 140%-179% of median income | 20% |
> | Development in any Waterfront district (RM-W, RL-W, DW) or 180% of median income and above in any other district | 25% |
>
> CITY OF BURLINGTON, VT., COMPREHENSIVE DEVELOPMENT ORDINANCE § 9.1.9 (2009)

Davidson's inclusionary zoning ordinance employs income tiering and provides examples of how inclusionary set-asides are calculated.

Distribution Table	
% of Area Median Income (AMI)	
Total Required Amount	12.5%
Very Low Income (Less than 50% of AMI)	30%–100%
Low Income (Between 50% and 80% of AMI)*	0%–70%
Moderate Income (Between 80% and 120% of AMI)	0%–20%
Middle Income (Between 120% and 150% of AMI)	0%–20%

Income limits can be exceeded by 10% upon approval of the Town Manager.

Example: A development with a total of 125 proposed units shall ensure that 16 of the 125 are affordable units (125 x .125 =16). In this example; no more than 109 units shall be market rate. (109 + 16 = 125) ... An example of possible distribution of these units:

> Required number of Affordable Units: 16
> Very Low Income Units: 30% x 16 = 4.8 rounded to 5
> Low Income Units: 30% x 16 = 4.8 rounded to 5
> Moderate Income Units: 20% x 16 = 3.2 rounded to 3
> Middle Income Units: 20% x 16 = 3.2 rounded to 3

Town of Davidson, N.C., Planning Ordinance § 6.3.2.C (2009)

Establishing Affordable Unit Prices

One of the core decisions for framers of an inclusionary zoning ordinance is establishing an "affordable" price for units set aside under an inclusionary zoning program. Inevitably this comes down to a policy decision about which households the ordinance is designed to help.

A housing needs assessment can help identify which households are in greatest need of housing affordable at their income level. For instance, some communities may be surprised to find that they have an adequate supply of housing for one segment of the workforce (for example, those earning 80 to 100 percent of the area median income) but an undersupply of housing affordable for another segment (for example, households earning 50 percent or less of the area median income). Given that information, framers could intentionally craft an inclusionary zoning ordinance to address the demonstrated shortage.

There are several steps to take in establishing an affordable price for inclusionary units:

1. Select a qualifying household income level—for what segments of the population should inclusionary units be affordable?
2. Define affordability—for a qualifying household (one with income at or below the established income level), what does it mean to say that a unit is affordable to that household?
3. Set maximum unit prices—this will generally be determined by the result of the first two steps, but some communities establish unit prices by reference to the cost of construction.

Each of these steps is discussed in detail below.

Selecting a Qualifying Household Income Level

The qualifying household income level is the maximum income a household may earn in order to qualify to purchase or rent an affordable unit produced under an inclusionary zoning program. In order to establish the threshold income level, the ordinance must reference some common source of public data that provides information about incomes within the community. Many communities rely on income limits established for Section 8 housing, because those figures are published regularly by the U.S. Department of Housing and Urban Development (HUD) and are accessible to the public via the HUD USER website.[31] Once the data standard is set, it becomes possible to discuss income levels by reference to that standard (for example, 80 percent of area median income, or 50 percent of the Section 8 income limit).

A variety of approaches may be used to establish the qualifying household income level. A simple approach is to establish a single income level and require all inclusionary units set aside under the inclusionary zoning program to be affordable to households earning less than the designated income. However, a number of communities employ sophisticated approaches in order to be more precise about which households are to benefit under the program and to give developers some flexibility in meeting affordability requirements. These other approaches fall into two categories, income tiering and income averaging.

Income tiering, which was discussed in "Set-Aside Percentage of Affordable Units," above, targets a percentage of the total inclusionary set-aside units to a specific range of incomes. For instance, a 15 percent affordable housing set-aside could be divided among two income groups, with the percentages set so as to target more precisely the affordability gaps in the housing stock (for example, 5 percent of the total number of units must be affordable to households earning less than 50 percent of area median income, and 10 percent must be affordable to households earning 50 to 80 percent of area median income). Some communities prefer the income tiering model because it can be used to achieve greater socioeconomic diversity within a single development.

Income averaging establishes a single target income, but it permits developers to price some units above the target level as long as other units are set at lower levels, such that the average price of all affordable units meets the target affordability level on average. This provides developers some measure of flexibility in meeting the affordability requirement.

EXAMPLES

Carrboro uses a single income level rather than a range or average.

> The appropriately-sized affordable housing unit must be offered for sale or rent at a price that does not exceed an amount that can be afforded by a family whose annual gross income equals 80 percent of the median gross annual family income, as most recently updated by the United States Department of Housing and Urban Development, for a family of a specific size within the Metropolitan Statistical Area where the Town of Carrboro is located.
>
> CARRBORO, N.C., TOWN CODE § 15-182.4(b)(1) (2009)

Manteo combines the income averaging and tiered approaches for its for-sale inclusionary units.

> *Income levels.* In covered development projects, at least one affordable housing unit or lot and no less than 50 percent of the affordable housing units or lots shall be sold to low-income households at a price that on average is affordable to a household with an annual income that is

65 percent of area median income for a household of four people in Dare County, North Carolina, as determined by the Section 8 Income Limits tables created annually by the United States Department of Housing and Urban Development (HUD). Any remaining affordable units or lots shall be sold to moderate-income households at a price that is affordable to a household with an annual income that is 80 percent of area median income for a household of four people in Dare County, North Carolina, as determined by the Section 8 Income Limits tables created annually by the United States Department of Housing and Urban Development (HUD).

TOWN OF MANTEO, N.C., ZONING CODE § 11-9 (2009)

Montgomery County provides for its qualifying household income level to be modified to ensure that first-year public school teachers will remain eligible for inclusionary units.

At the time the new income limits are set each year, the Department shall compare the maximum income needed to purchase for household size of one with the starting salary for a teacher (Bachelor degree) in the Montgomery County Public School System. If the Department determines that the maximum income figure under the Program would preclude the participation of a first year teacher in the school system, the Director may adjust the income limits accordingly to allow the participation of first year teachers.

MONTGOMERY COUNTY, MD., CODE REGS. (COMCOR) § 25A.00.02.02.2(e) (2003)

Defining Affordability

Once a qualifying household income level is established, unit prices are frequently based on what is affordable to households at that income level. The most commonly accepted definition of affordable housing, and the one frequently incorporated into inclusionary zoning ordinances, requires that a household spend no more than 30 percent of its income on housing.[32]

EXAMPLE

"Affordable housing" or "Affordable" shall refer to a housing [unit] . . . [for which] the total cost of the housing [unit] . . . is not more than thirty per cent (30%) of the household's gross annual income.

CITY OF BURLINGTON, VT., COMPREHENSIVE DEVELOPMENT ORDINANCE § 9.1.4 (2009)

Setting Unit Prices

Once decision makers have settled on the desired level of affordability for units produced under the program, the ordinance must set forth the method of calculating the maximum price of an inclusionary set-aside unit.

The process of setting rents for rental units is typically rather simple. In many inclusionary zoning ordinances, rental rates for inclusionary units are set at whatever has been defined as affordable for the households that will occupy the units; in other words, the price is a percentage of the target income level, regardless of costs of construction and maintenance (for example, maximum annual rent is 30 percent of the qualifying household income level). For rental units, some ordinances require utility costs and service fees to be included in the calculation of rent.

In North Carolina, this process is complicated somewhat by Section 42-14.1 of the North Carolina General Statutes (hereinafter G.S.), which prohibits regulating rent levels unless the property is owned by the city, county, or housing authority or the property is a subsidized unit operated pursuant to an agreement with the local government. Therefore, if a developer conveys units to the local government or a public agency or enters into an agreement on the control of rents, the inclusionary zoning program would fall into one of the exceptions.[33]

In the case of for-sale homes, the process for setting prices varies a bit more. Some municipalities simply require that the total cost of housing not exceed a percentage of the qualifying household income level, as seen above in the case of rental units. Others, like Montgomery County, include price formulae based on the cost of producing the home. Whatever method is used, some ordinances make adjustments for incidental costs of ownership, such as property taxes and homeowners association (HOA) or condominium fees, and for household size.

EXAMPLES

Dare County uses what is probably the simplest method for determining rental rates or sale prices for affordable housing set aside under its program. The cost of both rental and for-sale housing is simply pegged to the area median income for that year.

> 1. Family Housing: Housing for an eligible household which:
>   (i) Rents for a total annual amount at or below 30% of Median Family Income for Dare County, or
>   (ii) Sells at a price no more than three (3) times Median Family Income for Dare County.
>
> DARE COUNTY, N.C., ZONING ORDINANCE § 22-58.3(b) (2008)

Dare County's maximum price does not account for additional costs typically associated with owning a home, but San Diego's ordinance does.

> The sales price restrictions shall be established based on housing costs that do not exceed 35% of the annual median household income, including mortgage principal and interests [sic], taxes, insurance, HOA and assessments.
>
> CITY OF SAN DIEGO, CAL., INCLUSIONARY AFFORDABLE HOUS. IMPLEMENTATION & MONITORING PROCEDURES MANUAL 2 (revised Mar. 2008)

Napa, in calculating the affordable cost of a for-sale unit, likewise defines monthly housing expenses broadly.

> "Monthly owner-occupied housing payment" shall be that sum equal to the principal, interest, property taxes, homeowner's insurance and homeowner's association dues paid on an annual basis divided by 12.
>
> CITY OF NAPA, CAL., MUN. CODE § 15.94.020 (1999)

Burlington establishes that the maximum price of affordable for-sale units and rental units must include additional costs associated with ownership or rental, as appropriate.

"Affordable housing" or "Affordable" shall refer to a housing [unit] that is owned or rented by its inhabitants . . . the total cost of the housing, including principal, interest taxes and insurance and condominium association fees, if owned housing, or the total cost of the housing, including rent, utilities and condominium association fees, if rental housing, is not more than thirty per cent (30%) of the household's gross annual income.

CITY OF BURLINGTON, VT., COMPREHENSIVE DEVELOPMENT ORDINANCE § 9.1.4 (2009)

Montgomery County takes an altogether different approach. Rather than targeting the maximum price of an affordable home to a prospective purchaser's or renter's income level, Montgomery County bases the allowable price primarily on the estimated costs of construction. Montgomery County's highly detailed, multipart formula incorporates a number of factors to calculate the maximum acceptable price for sale of affordable housing units (MPDUs).[34]

(d) The following costs are included in the allowable sales price and are expressed as a percentage of the base sales price as follows:
  (1) Construction loan expenses—(prime rate + 2%) x .50 x .75 x .75. This assumes an average take down rate over 6 months, the length of the loan is 9 months, and that 75% of the unit sales price was borrowed;
  (2) Construction loan placement fee—1.5 percent;
  (3) Legal and closing costs—3.5 percent;
  (4) Marketing/Sales commission—1.5 percent;
  (5) Overhead—8 percent;
  (6) Engineering and architectural design fees—5 percent; and
  (7) General requirements (utilities, permits, etc.)—3 percent.
(e) The allowable sales price includes the following closing costs which are to be paid by the seller:
  (1) One-half of one percent for the permanent loan origination fee;
  (2) County tax certificate, transfer charges, revenue stamps and recordation charges;
  (3) Title examination, settlement, and attorney fees;
  (4) Notary fees and fees for preparation of a deed of conveyance, a deed of trust or mortgage, and the deed of trust or mortgage note;

(5) Appraisal fee and credit report fee; and

(6) House location survey plat.

(f) The maximum allowable sales price for new MPDUs sold to the Commission or to an eligible non-profit must be reduced by 1.5 percent to reflect the reduced sales and marketing costs associated with these units.

(g) Fees required to place permanent financing that are paid by the seller must be permitted to be added to the allowable sales price to determine the final sales price to the purchaser. These fees may include the seller's permanent loan fees (points) which are in excess of one-half percent and any buy-down fees paid to a financial institution to reduce mortgage interest rates on the purchaser's loan below current market interest rates. There must be no additions if the buyer secures their own permanent financing.

. . .

(i) Water and sewer house connection fees are not included in the calculation of the MPDU base sales price. In any instance where water and sewer connection charges are not deferred, the allowable sales price may be adjusted to reflect this increased cost to the seller.

. . .

(k) When a gas heating and air-conditioning (HVAC) system is substituted for an electrical heat pump in an MPDU, the allowable sales price may be adjusted by the Department to compensate for this expense.

(l) When the buyer and seller of an MPDU agree to modify the unit structurally to facilitate access or use by a person with mobility or sensory impairments, the Department may adjust the allowable sales price by the amount of the additional costs. The Applicant must obtain approval of the price from the Department prior to executing a sales contract.

(m) The Department may adjust the allowable sales price of an MPDU if the applicant can demonstrate that additional unusual costs have been incurred (i.e., costs not already included in the allowable structure or lot development costs) which are directly attributable to and benefit the MPDUs and which are the result of:

(1) Conditions or fees imposed by a government agency or as a condition for building permit approval;

(2) Additional considerations for fees as a condition of obtaining government financing programs; or

(3) Additional fees or costs imposed by public utilities.

Documentation for such costs must accompany the sales offering agreement submitted to the Department. Requests for price adjustments must be initiated by the applicant.

. . .

(o) The loan amount, but not the final sales price, shall be increased to cover the cost of amortizing the mortgage insurance premium on Federal Housing Administration (FHA) and Commission/FHA loans.

(p) The maximum, allowable sales prices of MPDUs must be revised annually by June 15 of each year by adjusting the prior year's maximum prices by the percentage change in the consumer price index for urban consumers (CPI-U) for the Washington Metropolitan Area for the preceding 12 month period. Alternately, the prices may be re-estimated using actual current prices and costs, or through the use of commercially available standard building industry cost estimating products. Interim adjustments in the maximum sales prices may be made when a change in the relevant cost elements of the CPI-U for the Washington Metropolitan Area exceeds 2 percent, or when significant changes in government or other costs are imposed between periods of price adjustment.

MONTGOMERY COUNTY, MD., CODE REGS. (COMCOR) § 25A.00.02.05.1 (2003)

Burlington sets income levels for different-sized units based on published income figures for different household sizes.

In calculating the rents or carrying charges of inclusionary units, the following relationship between unit size and household size shall apply:

TABLE INSET:

Unit Size	Household Size Equivalent
Efficiency Units:	[HUD-published figure for a] 1 Person Household;
One-Bedroom Units:	1.5 Person Household (average of one and two-person household incomes);
Two-Bedroom Units:	3 Person Household;
Three-Bedroom Units:	4.5 Person Household (average of four and five-person household incomes);
Four-Bedroom Units:	6 Person Household.

CITY OF BURLINGTON, VT., COMPREHENSIVE DEVELOPMENT ORDINANCE § 9.1.12(c) (2009)

Notes

1. ENTERPRISE COMMUNITY PARTNERS, INCLUSIONARY ZONING: PROGRAM DESIGN CONSIDERATIONS 2–3 (2004).

2. This chapter addresses some of the major legal issues associated with each approach. For a fuller discussion of local government authority to enact inclusionary zoning, see "Local Government Authority to Enact Inclusionary Zoning in North Carolina" in the Legal Appendix.

3. See "Managing Inclusionary Units" in Chapter 7.

4. BUSINESS AND PROFESSIONAL PEOPLE FOR THE PUBLIC INTEREST, OPENING THE DOOR TO INCLUSIONARY ZONING 6 (2003) (hereinafter BPI).

5. Douglas R. Porter, *The Promise and Practice of Inclusionary Zoning, in* GROWTH MANAGEMENT AND AFFORDABLE HOUSING: DO THEY CONFLICT? 218–19 (Anthony Downs ed., 2004). See also "Impacts on the Broader Housing Market" in Chapter 1.

6. Incentives are discussed in Chapter 4.

7. For a general examination of takings analysis in the context of inclusionary zoning, see "Takings" in the Legal Appendix.

8. Reasonableness is a key factor in evaluating due process claims, takings claims, and authority under the police power. See the Legal Appendix for a more detailed treatment of this point.

9. For a detailed analysis of implied authority, see "Local Government Authority to Enact Inclusionary Zoning in North Carolina" in the Legal Appendix.

10. *See, e.g.,* Union Land Owners Ass'n v. County of Union, ___ N.C. App. ___, 689 S.E.2d 504 (2009) (interpreting zoning, subdivision, and police powers narrowly in the school impact fee context).

11. In both the 2001–2 and 2003–4 sessions of the North Carolina General Assembly, bills were introduced on behalf of communities in the Research Triangle region of the state seeking authority to enact mandatory inclusionary zoning ordinances. S. 1001 (2001); S. 493 (2003). Neither of the bills survived its respective legislative committee assignment. Such action could indicate opposition to granting the authority, or it might simply mean that the legislature believed at the time that such authority already existed.

12. CENTER FOR AFFORDABLE LIVING, TRIANGLE VOLUNTARY DENSITY BONUSES FOR AFFORDABLE HOUSING (Triangle J Council of Governments 2001).

13. *See* N.C. GEN. STAT. (hereinafter G.S.) §§ 153A-340, 153A-345, 160A-381, 160A-388. *See also* DAVID W. OWENS, LAND USE LAW IN NORTH CAROLINA 121–28 (UNC School of Government 2006).

14. *See* OWENS, note 13 above, at 122–24.

15. G.S. 160A-382(a) and 153A-342(a). *See also* OWENS, note 13 above, at 95–98.

16. *See* G.S. 160A-382. *See also* OWENS, note 13 above, at 98. As a matter of U.S. constitutional law, dedications of property required as a condition of land use approval must be related to and roughly proportional to the impact of the expected use. Nollan v. Cal. Coastal Comm'n, 483 U.S. 825 (1987); Dolan v. City of Tigard, 512 U.S. 374 (1994). See also "Takings" in the Legal Appendix.

17. For a discussion of how to use a needs assessment for this purpose, see "Conducting a Housing Needs Assessment" in Chapter 1.

18. For an example of a legislative finding along these lines and other findings made in support of inclusionary zoning conditions, see "Findings" in Chapter 2.

19. Case law regarding tenancy controls often refers to a distinction based on tenancy as the "manner of ownership," but the terms are interchangeable.

20. Relief mechanisms, such as hardship clauses, are discussed in greater detail in Chapter 5.

21. Philip B. Herr, *Zoning for Affordability in Massachusetts: An Overview, in* 2 NATIONAL HOUSING CONFERENCE AFFORDABLE HOUSING POLICY REVIEW: INCLUSIONARY ZONING: LESSONS LEARNED IN MASSACHUSETTS 3, 5 (2002), *available at* www.nhc.org/media/documents/IZ_lessons_in_MA.pdf.

22. *See* CITY OF BURLINGTON, VT., COMPREHENSIVE DEVELOPMENT ORDINANCE § 9.1.5 (2009), *available at* www.ci.burlington.vt.us/planning/zoning/zn_ordinance/article_09_housing.pdf ("Multiple developments or projects by the same applicant or responsible party within any consecutive twelve (12) month period that in the aggregate equal or exceed the [size threshold for covered developments] shall be subject to these regulations.").

23. CITY OF NAPA, CAL., MUN. CODE § 15.94.040 (2005). *See also* Nico Calavita, *Origins and Evolution of Inclusionary Housing in California, in* 3 NATIONAL HOUSING CONFERENCE AFFORDABLE HOUSING POLICY REVIEW: INCLUSIONARY ZONING: THE CALIFORNIA EXPERIENCE 3, 6 (2004), *available at* www.nhc.org/media/documents/IZ_CA_experiencet.pdf ("It is generally accepted that a healthy balance between jobs and housing mandates one new residential unit for every 1.5 jobs created.").

24. Inclusionary housing fees for nonresidential developments may be subject to increased scrutiny in North Carolina. See the discussion of *Union Land Owners Ass'n v. County of Union* and possible distinctions from inclusionary zoning under "In-Lieu Payments" in Chapter 5, and "Local Government Authority to Enact Inclusionary Zoning in North Carolina" in the Legal Appendix.

25. Although North Carolina law would allow an inclusionary zoning ordinance to apply to a property undergoing a change in use (e.g., a conversion of a commercial warehouse into residential condominiums), the law appears not to allow inclusionary zoning to be applied to a change in ownership (e.g., a conversion from tenant-occupied apartments to owner-occupied condominiums while leaving the building's residential use essentially unchanged). See the discussion of *Graham Court Associates v. Town Council of Town of Chapel Hill*, 53 N.C. App. 543, 546–47, 281 S.E.2d 418, 420 (1981) under "Change in Tenancy," below.

26. *See, e.g.,* SANTA FE, N.M., CITY CODE § 26-1.8 (1) (2009) ("The SFHP [Santa Fe Homes Program] applies to new construction and to the conversion of existing rental units to ownership units."); CITY OF SAN DIEGO, CAL., MUN. CODE § 142.1306(c) (2008) ("Condominium conversions of twenty or more dwelling units shall satisfy the requirement to provide dwelling units affordable to and occupied by targeted rental households or targeted ownership households on the same site as the condominium conversion project").

27. A panel of the North Carolina Court of Appeals, in *Graham Court Associates v. Town Council of Town of Chapel Hill*, ruled that a local government could not use its zon-

ing authority to require a property owner to obtain a special use permit in order to convert apartments into condominiums, as the conversion represented a change in "manner of ownership" rather than a change in "use" of the property. The court drew a distinction between the use of property (e.g., commercial versus residential) and the manner of ownership of property (e.g., rental tenancy versus condominium ownership by occupants) and decided that zoning regulation is permitted for the former but not for the latter. As the court put it, "If a *use* is permitted . . . it is beyond the power of the municipality to regulate the *manner of ownership* of the legal estate." Graham Court Assocs. v. Town Council of Town of Chapel Hill, 53 N.C. App. 543, 551, 281 S.E.2d 418, 422–23 (1981) (emphasis added). See also the discussion of *Wilmington v. Hill* under "Consistent Tenancy or Manner of Ownership" in Chapter 6.

28. *See* Jenny Schuetz, Rachel Meltzer, and Vicki Been, *31 Flavors of Inclusionary Zoning: Comparing Policies from San Francisco, Washington, DC, and Suburban Boston*, 75 Journal of the American Planning Association 441 (2009).

29. Reasonableness and a connection between ends and means are key factors to be considered in legal challenges questioning whether an ordinance complies with due process or is a legitimate exercise of government authority. The applicable tests are described in the "Takings," "Due Process," and "Local Government Authority to Enact Inclusionary Zoning in North Carolina" sections of the Legal Appendix.

30. Burlington's system for assigning set-aside percentages seems to place a greater burden on developments with higher-priced housing. Prior to following the Burlington model, communities may need to establish a rational basis for making a distinction based on the average house price of a development. A rational basis for such a system might be supported by data indicating that developers in the community earn higher profit margins at higher housing price points (as is often the case) and therefore the burden on profitability is actually proportionally the same across all developments. It might also be supported by data indicating that higher-priced developments tend to generate a greater amount of related commercial development (designed to serve residents of the higher-priced development) employing lower-wage employees, thereby justifying a greater affordable set-aside for those higher-priced developments.

31. HUD USER's data sets and income data for specific counties and rent markets are accessible through links at www.huduser.org/datasets/il.html.

32. *See* U.S. Department of Housing and Urban Development, Affordable Housing, www.hud.gov/offices/cpd/affordablehousing/.

33. For a more complete discussion of the issues surrounding rent control statutes, see "North Carolina Limitation on Rent Control" in the Legal Appendix.

34. A similar calculus is applied for pricing of rental units. *See* Montgomery County, Md., Code Regs. (COMCOR) § 25A.00.02.05.2 (2003).

4

Incentives

Along with the basic requirement for units to be set aside for affordable housing, one of the key elements of any inclusionary zoning ordinance is the collection of incentives offered to offset some of the costs of providing housing units at below-market rates. The primary purpose of incentives in an inclusionary zoning program—whether participation is voluntary or mandatory—is to encourage developers to supply more units or lower-priced units than would otherwise be the case.[1]

There may also be a legal reason for providing incentives, though it is not a primary consideration. Incentives may have some influence in a judicial determination of whether an inclusionary zoning program amounts to a taking of the owner's property for the common good, for which the owner must be compensated.[2] Even without incentives in place, it would be difficult for a takings claim to prevail against an inclusionary zoning program. United States Supreme Court case law indicates that a taking occurs only when there is a physical occupation of property[3] or when the owner is deprived of all economically beneficial use of the whole property.[4] In fact, no state or federal court has concluded that inclusionary zoning set-asides amount to a taking under federal law, even in the case of mandatory programs. This suggests that incentives are not necessary to defeat a takings claim. Nonetheless, in at least one case, the presence of incentives proved helpful to a court in dismissing a takings claim.[5]

The most common incentives appearing in the surveyed inclusionary zoning ordinances include the following:

- Density bonuses
- Fee reductions or waivers
- Fast-tracking of permit applications
- Relaxation of other development standards

Each of these incentives is discussed below.

Since incentives are typically designed to motivate developers in the local community, it may also be wise to ask developers directly what incentives would motivate them most and what incentives would be most effective at offsetting any cost of producing below-market housing. Ensuring that the development community understands the incentives and has a voice in shaping the options and incentives could help improve cooperation with the inclusionary zoning program and enhance its effectiveness.

Density Bonuses

Density bonuses allow a developer to build more units than the zoning or subdivision ordinance would normally allow. One thing to keep in mind when considering a density bonus is the impact that the additional housing units will have. Can the municipality's infrastructure handle 5 percent or 10 percent more units in a given development? Are residents apprehensive about greater density in the community? Will density bonuses conflict with environmental protection policies?

In North Carolina, local governments are permitted to regulate "the *density* of population, and the location and use of buildings," among other things.[6] It seems, therefore, that the plain text of the statute authorizes the use of density bonuses.[7] Indeed, the statute specifically permits a local government to award density bonuses to developers for providing dedicated rights-of-way[8] and for enhancing energy efficiency.[9] The fact that the General Assembly authorized density bonuses for those specific purposes and failed to mention other purposes does not necessarily preclude local governments from enacting density bonuses for purposes not explicitly mentioned.[10] To avoid any ambiguity, however, several local governments have obtained special legislation to permit the enactment of density bonuses as an incentive for the voluntary production of affordable housing.[11]

EXAMPLES

Manteo offers one of the highest density bonuses in North Carolina, a one-to-one bonus for each inclusionary unit.

For all covered developments under this chapter, a density bonus shall be provided equal to one market rate unit or lot for each affordable housing unit or lot. Under no circumstances may a single-family lot contain less than 6,000 square feet unless approved by both the planning board and the town Board of Commissioners.

TOWN OF MANTEO, N.C., ZONING CODE § 11-5 (2009)

In providing density bonuses to developers who are not subject to mandatory set-aside requirements, Fairfax County offers greater density bonuses for single-family units than for multifamily units, a practice that may encourage developers to build more affordable single-family units.

5. Affordable dwelling units may be provided, at the developer's option, in any residential development in the R-2 through R-30 and P Districts which is not required to provide affordable dwelling units pursuant to the provisions of this Part. Such development shall be subject to the applicable zoning district regulations for affordable dwelling unit developments and shall be in accordance with the following:

    A. For single family detached and single family attached dwelling unit developments, there may be a potential density bonus of up to twenty (20) percent, provided that not less than twelve and one-half (12.5) percent of the total number of dwelling units are provided as affordable dwelling units, subject to the provisions of this Part.

    B. For multiple family dwelling unit structures that do not have an elevator, or have an elevator and are three (3) stories or less in height, there may be a potential density bonus for the development consisting of such structures of up to ten (10) percent, provided that not less than six and one-quarter (6.25) percent of the total number of dwelling units are provided as affordable dwelling units, or a potential density bonus for the development consisting of such structures from greater than ten (10) percent up to twenty (20) percent, provided that not less than twelve and one-half (12.5) percent of the total number of dwelling units are provided as affordable dwelling units, subject to the provisions of this Part.

C. For multiple family dwelling unit structures that have an elevator and are four (4) stories or more in height, there may be a potential density bonus for the development consisting of such structures of up to seventeen (17) percent, provided that not less than six and one-quarter (6.25) percent of the total number of dwelling units are provided as affordable dwelling units, subject to the provisions of this Part for multiple family dwelling developments with fifty (50) percent or less of the required parking provided in parking structures. For such multiple family developments with more than fifty (50) percent of the required parking provided in parking structures, there may be a potential density bonus of up to seventeen (17) percent, provided that not less than five (5) percent of the total number of dwelling units are provided as affordable dwelling units, subject to the provisions of this Part.

COUNTY OF FAIRFAX, VA., ZONING ORDINANCE § 2-802 (2009)

Fee Reductions and Waivers

Offsets for a variety of fees—for example, permitting, inspection, and utility connection fees—are a common element of inclusionary zoning laws. In North Carolina, the method for instituting fees and awarding waivers requires some additional sensitivity to state law.

Local governments in North Carolina are authorized to institute "reasonable" fees to cover the costs of implementing regulatory programs, such as permit review and approvals, building inspections, and the like.[12] However, North Carolina law prohibits local governments from charging similarly situated customers different utility rates or fees for public enterprises, such as water and sewer service, unless there is a usage- or business-related reason for the difference.[13] For example, a local government might be able to justify a lower water line *maintenance* fee for affordable housing units with fewer bathrooms than their market-rate counterparts as a usage-related difference, but it would be much more difficult to develop a business rationale for differences in utility *connection* fees.

This suggests that North Carolina local governments should exercise care in designing fee offsets. Rather than instituting fee waivers, which might be viewed as setting different rates for similarly situated customers, many local governments take a more cautious approach by offering fee reimbursements. Under this approach, a local government assesses and collects standard fees—such as utility fees for its enterprise fund—and then separately authorizes reimbursements for those fees out of the general fund. Payment of fee reimbursements is permitted pursuant to a local government's broad authority to provide for the construction of housing for low- and moderate-income persons.[14]

EXAMPLE

Manteo's fee waivers are termed "development cost offsets." Note that waivers are not granted for water or wastewater fees, as these are utility fees that, in North Carolina, may not be waived for nonbusiness reasons.

> An applicant who fully complies with the requirements of this chapter shall, upon written request, receive from the town, with regard to the affordable housing units or lots in the covered development, a waiver of all of the otherwise applicable application fees, building permit fees, plan review fees, inspection fees, and such other development fees and costs which may be imposed by the town, except for any fees associated with water or wastewater which shall be charged at market rates.
>
> Town of Manteo, N.C., Zoning Code § 11-7 (2009)

Fast-Track Permitting

For builders and developers, time is money, as interest charges, loan repayments, and other carrying costs accumulate every day. Developers obtain measurable monetary value by avoiding permitting delays,[15] so a faster approval process for developments supplying inclusionary units can be a powerful incentive. The faster approval process could strictly limit the maximum number of days in which an expedited review must be completed,[16] or it could consist of a separate review process that can be completed in less time than the usual process. Perhaps the most important consideration in fast-track permitting is ensuring that the local planning department is adequately staffed to process development applications quickly without sacrificing thoroughness.

Sacramento offers a separate approval process in which its planning director holds authority to issue special permits for developments containing inclusionary units. It also offers priority processing of permits for inclusionary housing developments.

> Streamlining and Priority Processing. The planning director may issue special permits for residential projects that include an inclusionary housing component. The city shall develop further procedures for streamlining and priority processing which relieve inclusionary units of permit processing requirements to the maximum extent feasible consistent with the public health, safety and welfare.
>
> SACRAMENTO, CAL., CITY CODE § 17.190.040.D (2009)

Relaxed Development Standards

Partly because developments covered by inclusionary zoning laws are generally built at greater densities, local governments may offer relaxation of other development standards such as lot size and parking requirements. Even in a municipality that offers no density bonuses, granting relaxed setback or lot size requirements may allow developers to build more units than otherwise possible. Still, communities should be mindful of policy goals and ensure that relaxation of development standards does not unreasonably interfere with other policy priorities.

Some inclusionary zoning ordinances relax standards by delegating discretion over development standards to planning staff. In North Carolina, such delegation could be unlawful.[17] To comply with North Carolina law, any discretion may be vested only in a quasi-judicial board such as a zoning board of adjustment, and even then, that board must be provided adequate standards to guide its judgment.[18]

Chapel Hill's new ordinance allows for reductions in the minimum lot size in order to accommodate additional lots as part of a density bonus.

> For subdivisions, if the applicant elects to use a density bonus, the minimum lot size required by [the base zoning requirement] may be reduced by up to 25% to accommodate the additional lots.
>
> CODE OF ORDINANCES OF THE TOWN OF CHAPEL HILL § 3.10.2(d)(2) (2010)

An earlier draft of this ordinance provided for the relaxation of other development standards in zoning districts that are not subject to density restrictions and thus do not have a base maximum density to which a bonus could be applied.

> (d) Development Bonus for Single-Family Dwelling Units
>
> . . .
>
> (2) For residential subdivisions or other applications that request approval and are not subject to maximum density restrictions [that is, units in a zoning district without a density limit], the development bonus is established by reduction in lot size requirements as follows:
>
> A. Subtracting land area proposed as right-of-way and required parks and open space . . . from the total area of the proposed subdivision. For purposes of this subsection, the total subdivision area shall be reduced by 15% for right-of-way unless that applicant demonstrates that actual right-of-way for streets and utilities is less than the assumed amount; and
>
> B. Dividing this amount by the minimum lot size to determine the maximum number of dwelling units normally permitted; and
>
> C. Multiplying the maximum number of dwelling units allowed in the zoning district . . . by the density bonus percentage [provided by this inclusionary zoning ordinance].
>
> TOWN OF CHAPEL HILL DRAFT INCLUSIONARY ZONING ORDINANCE § 3.10.2 (as presented Mar. 15, 2010)

Fairfax County's ordinance does not apply its standard regulations for bulk, unit type, lot size, and open space to inclusionary developments.

> Any development which provides affordable dwelling units on site and/or which includes bonus market rate dwelling units on site [*i.e.*, any development which has received a density bonus] pursuant to the provisions of this Part, shall comply with the respective zoning district regulations which apply to affordable dwelling unit developments.
>
> COUNTY OF FAIRFAX, VA., ZONING ORDINANCE § 2-805 (2009)

A separate article (Article 3) of the Fairfax County Zoning Ordinance then sets forth separate lot size, yard, and open space requirements for each residential zoning classification that are less stringent for inclusionary developments than for other developments.

Sacramento's inclusionary housing ordinance provides additional discretion to various authorities with regard to planning and development standards (assignment of such discretion in a North Carolina ordinance would need to comply with North Carolina law).

> Modification of Planning and Public Works Development Standards. Upon application as provided herein, the city may modify for inclusionary units, to the extent feasible in light of the uses, design, and infrastructure needs of the development project as determined by the planning director, the zoning administrator, or planning commission, as applicable under the city zoning code: (1) applicable public works development standards contained in Titles 12 and 16 of the city code, such as alternative standards relating to road widths, curbs and gutters, and parking; and (2) applicable planning standards contained elsewhere in this title such as minimum lot size, alternative housing types, and other minor deviations from development standards, lot coverage, locational and other requirements for approval of duplexes, halfplexes, and patio homes.
>
> SACRAMENTO, CAL., CITY CODE § 17.190.040.B (2009)

Notes

1. *See* CALIFORNIA AFFORDABLE HOUSING LAW PROJECT & WESTERN CENTER ON LAW AND POVERTY, INCLUSIONARY ZONING: POLICY CONSIDERATIONS AND BEST PRACTICES 6 (2002).

2. *See* U.S. CONST. amend. V ("nor shall private property be taken for public use, without just compensation").

3. Loretto v. Teleprompter Manhattan CATV Corp., 458 U.S. 419, 434–35 (1982) ("... when the 'character of the governmental action' is a permanent physical occupation of property, our cases uniformly have found a taking to the extent of the occupation, without regard to whether the action achieves an important public benefit or has only minimal economic impact on the owner." (citation omitted)).

4. *See* Lucas v. S.C. Coastal Council, 505 U.S. 1003, 1019 (1992) ("[W]hen the owner of real property has been called upon to sacrifice all economically beneficial uses in the name of the common good ... he has suffered a taking."); Concrete Pipe & Prods. v. Constr. Laborers Pension Trust, 508 U.S. 602, 644 (1993) (applying the *Lucas* test for deprivation of all economically beneficial use of the property to the whole property, not merely the regulated portion of it). North Carolina has its own strain of takings law, but it is not substantially different. For a fuller discussion of federal and North Carolina takings law, see "Takings" in the Legal Appendix.

5. Home Builders Ass'n of N. Cal. v. City of Napa, 90 Cal. App. 4th 188, 194 (2001) ("Here, City's inclusionary zoning ordinance imposes significant burdens on those who wish to develop their property. However the ordinance also provides significant benefits to those who comply with its terms.").

6. N.C. GEN. STAT. (hereinafter G.S.) §§ 153A-340 and 160A-381 (emphasis added).

7. G.S. 153A-340 (counties) and 160A-381 (cities).

8. *Id.*

9. G.S. 160A-384.

10. Homebuilders Ass'n of Charlotte, Inc. v. City of Charlotte, 336 N.C. 37, 45, 442 S.E.2d 45, 51 (1994) ("... the Court of Appeals noted that the General Assembly has expressly authorized county water and sewer districts to charge user fees for furnished services while it has remained silent on the authority to impose user fees for other services. Here again, the General Assembly did not specify that sewer services were the only services for which user fees could be charged and we find no basis for such a strained reading of this statute."). *But cf.* Union Land Owners Ass'n v. County of Union, ___ N.C. App. ___, 689 S.E.2d 504 (2009) (holding that a zoning ordinance "must use the tools authorized by the zoning statute").

11. *See, e.g.*, An Act Amending the Charter of the City of Wilmington to Authorize Zoning Density Bonuses in Projects Containing Specified Amounts of Low and Moderate Income Housing, 1991 N.C. Sess. Laws ch. 119; An Act Concerning Zoning by the City of Winston-Salem and Forsyth County, 1993 N.C. Sess. Laws ch. 588; An Act to Make Various Amendments to Laws Applicable to Orange and Chatham Counties, 1991 N.C. Sess. Laws ch. 246.

12. Homebuilders Ass'n of Charlotte, Inc. v. City of Charlotte, 336 N.C. 37, 46, 442 S.E.2d 45, 50 (1994) (concluding that a city has authority to assess user fees for a variety of governmental regulatory services and for the use of public facilities, provided such fees are reasonable).

13. For a complete discussion of the law surrounding utility rates, see Kara A. Millonzi, *Lawful Discrimination in Utility Ratemaking*, LOCAL FINANCE BULLETIN No. 33 (October 2006), *available at* www.sog.unc.edu/pubs/electronicversions/pdfs/lfb33.pdf.

14. G.S. 157-9 grants sweeping authority to housing authorities to provide for the construction of affordable housing, and G.S. 153A-376(b) and 160A-456(b) extend that authority to counties and cities.

15. DAVID N. AMMONS, RYAN A. DAVIDSON, AND RYAN M. EWALT, DEVELOPMENT REVIEW IN LOCAL GOVERNMENT: BENCHMARKING BEST PRACTICES 28 (UNC School of Government 2009) (describing an instance in which developers accepted a 70 percent hike in permitting fees in exchange for a promise by a local government that permits would be approved within a specified time frame 90 percent of the time).

16. Denver, Colorado, enacted an inclusionary zoning ordinance that establishes a 180-day time limit in which expedited planning department review must be completed. *See* CITY & COUNTY OF DENVER, COLO., REV. MUN. CODE § 27-108 (2009).

17. *See* DAVID W. OWENS, LAND USE LAW IN NORTH CAROLINA 121–24 (UNC School of Government 2006).

18. *Id.*

5

Flexibility Measures

When compliance is optional, as with a voluntary inclusionary zoning program, there is no need to enact flexible alternatives to compliance, because opting out is always an available alternative for the developer.

Similarly, conditional programs are inherently flexible due to the negotiation process undertaken prior to approval, but the flexibility is not unbounded. As a matter of U.S. constitutional law, dedications of property required as a condition of land use approval must be related to and roughly proportional to the impact of the expected use.[1] Under North Carolina law, any conditions or site-specific standards imposed must be limited to those that address the impacts reasonably expected to be generated by the development.[2]

In the case of a mandatory program, flexibility must be intentionally designed into the program to avoid harsh or legally problematic results, as well as to encourage creativity and to respond to unusual circumstances. These flexibility measures come in three basic forms:

- Prospective application clauses to account for projects already in progress at the effective date of the inclusionary zoning ordinance
- Hardship clauses to address situations in which providing affordable housing units would be difficult or impossible
- Alternatives to on-site development to permit developers to comply through means other than on-site construction

Each measure is discussed below. Whether flexibility measures are enacted as part of a mandatory program or incorporated into negotiations in a conditional program, it is advisable to consult with a local government attorney regarding their application.

Prospective Application Clauses

Prospective application clauses ensure that an ordinance applies only prospectively by explicitly permitting projects to go forward if they were already approved or in progress at the effective date of the inclusionary zoning ordinance. The legal purpose is to eliminate two concerns with retroactive application of legislation. First, retroactive regulations present serious problems of unfairness that raise due process concerns.[3] Second, retroactive regulations may interfere with a property owner's common law vested rights[4] or investment-backed expectations.[5] Prospective application clauses eliminate these concerns.

Prospective application clauses typically include a date after which development applications will be subject to the inclusionary zoning ordinance, and for applications received prior to that date (and therefore not subject to the ordinance), a date by which buildings must be constructed (or provided certificates of occupancy) in order to avoid being subject to the ordinance. As an alternative, a prospective application clause can simply restate current North Carolina law on vested rights within its terms.[6]

EXAMPLE

Boulder's prospective application clause requires developments approved prior to enactment of the inclusionary zoning ordinance to be completed by a certain date in order to remain exempt from the ordinance.

(e) Transition to Inclusionary Zoning Requirements: Developments [of the type covered by the ordinance] shall be permitted to develop utilizing no more than one of the following provisions:

    (1) Developments Approved Prior to 1995: Developments which received development plan approvals prior to October 5, 1995, shall conform to the provisions of this chapter or, in the alternative, may develop in compliance with the conditions of their previously issued development plan approvals so long as the construction of dwelling units are completed by December 31, 2001.

CITY OF BOULDER, COLO., REV. CODE § 9-13-3 (2009)

Hardship Clauses and Variances

Even when an inclusionary zoning ordinance is limited to prospective application, there may be circumstances particular to an individual development in which compliance with inclusionary zoning requirements may severely diminish the value of that development to the point that the developer's original plan is no longer feasible. In such a case, the developer might claim that his or her property has been subject to a taking that requires just compensation (recall, however, that to be a taking, the effect of the regulation generally must be to deprive the owner of all economically beneficial use of his or her property taken as a whole).[7] A clause that allows developers to obtain reductions or waivers from the inclusionary zoning ordinance in such circumstances can be helpful, and in the case of Napa, such a clause was determinative in overcoming a takings challenge to a mandatory inclusionary zoning ordinance.[8]

Hardship clauses are designed to address situations in which a developer would be forced to take a loss on the property or in which all economically viable use of the property would be eliminated. Other possible elements of a hardship clause include the following:

- A requirement that the owner provide reasonable evidence to prove a hardship (in order to reduce the likelihood of frivolous claims)
- A catchall that would allow for flexibility in other situations that could result in a taking (as each development has its own unique set of circumstances)

In most states, hardship cases are addressed through variances. In North Carolina, boards of adjustment have the power to vary or modify the requirements of a zoning ordinance when practical difficulties or unnecessary hardships would result.[9]

EXAMPLE

Santa Fe's hardship clause addresses the takings concern and includes both of the other elements mentioned above. Subsection (a) of the ordinance's definition of "extreme hardship" addresses takings directly. Subsection (b) requires that the property owner be able to demonstrate that the loss would be an *unavoidable* consequence of the inclusionary zoning requirement, thus ensuring that developers use creative means at their disposal to avoid losses and limiting the number of qualifying cases. Subsection (c) functions as a catchall to address any other possible takings claims.

> *Extreme hardship* means a condition occurring as a direct consequence of the [inclusionary zoning] Ordinance which: (a) deprives a property owner of all economically viable use of the subject property taken as a whole; or (b) would require the property owner to lose money on the development taken as a whole and the property owner can demonstrate to the governing body's satisfaction that said loss would be an unavoidable consequence of the [inclusionary zoning] requirement for construction of [affordable housing] units; or (c) the property owner can demonstrate to the council's satisfaction that complying with the requirements of this chapter would constitute taking property in violation of the Constitution of the United States or New Mexico.
>
> SANTA FE, N.M., CITY CODE § 26-1.5 (2009)

Alternatives to On-Site Development

Some inclusionary zoning programs require inclusionary housing units to be built on the same site as the market-rate development that triggered the requirement. On-site provision is seen as a way to ensure that households in affordable units have access to employment centers, transportation, activities, social support systems, and services normally located near market-rate developments.[10] However, there may be circumstances in which a developer does not qualify for relief under a hardship clause, but a local government nevertheless agrees that on-site development of affordable housing is not appropriate or should not be required. In these cases, ordinances typically require that the applicant show, or that the local government find, that certain factors apply before an alternative to on-site compliance may be employed. Typical circumstances that qualify for exceptions to on-site building requirements include the following:

- The advantages of co-location are not present (for example, the market-rate development will be placed far from employment centers, transportation, and other services), and therefore low-income and/or special-needs housing units would be better provided at another location.

- On-site provision would cause a recognizable economic hardship (possibly because the site is on extremely expensive land or the site topography makes constructing the requisite number of homes difficult).

The most common alternatives to on-site construction of inclusionary units are the following:

- Off-site provision, whereby inclusionary units are built at a different location from the site of the development to which the requirements are applied
- In-lieu payments, whereby the developer donates funds to a local government agency, a nonprofit organization, or a housing authority for future construction or acquisition of affordable housing
- Land donation, whereby the developer donates land to a local government or qualifying nonprofit organization, which is to be used for future construction of affordable housing

In each case, the alternatives are structured to provide the local government with approximately the same value it would receive if the inclusionary units were constructed on-site. While these alternatives are meant to provide flexibility, they may appear similar in form to an exaction, which is the surrender of rights or property by a landowner as a condition of a land use approval.[11] It is therefore possible that a court could evaluate such alternatives under an exactions analysis developed by the U.S. Supreme Court that examines whether the exactions are related to and roughly proportional to the impacts of the proposed development.[12] North Carolina courts have applied a similar rule requiring exactions to have a "rational nexus" to the needs created by the development.[13] Accordingly, it is advisable to keep any alternatives to on-site compliance tied as closely as possible to the loss of on-site inclusionary units that otherwise would have been provided.[14]

In North Carolina, the primary concern about such alternative forms of compliance is the authority for offering them to developers. Under a conditional inclusionary zoning program, local governments possess ample authority to negotiate with developers with respect to alternative forms of compliance, provided that the negotiated alternative complies with the limitations on exactions described above.[15] Authority is less clear, however, in a mandatory program.

Although North Carolina local governments have been granted authority to require dedications of land or fees for certain purposes, such as rights-of-way for streets and fees for recreation, there is no explicit authority to require the dedication of land or the payment of fees for affordable housing as an alternative to compliance with a land use ordinance's requirement.[16] So while North Carolina local governments arguably possess authority to require a mix of affordability in residential developments through inclusionary zoning,they may not have sufficient authority to offer alternatives to compliance. [17]

Off-Site Provision

Some ordinances allow developers to choose where to provide the affordable units, while others do not allow off-site provision at all.

EXAMPLES

Manteo requires on-site provision of all inclusionary units.

> *General requirement.* Except as otherwise specifically provided, 20 percent of the total number of residential units or lots within any covered development shall be affordable housing units or lots and shall be located on the site of the covered development.
>
> TOWN OF MANTEO, N.C., ZONING CODE § 11-3(a) (2009)

San Diego requires a developer to obtain a variance in order to provide housing off site and will approve the off-site construction only if it meets other goals of the city.

> (f) A project that proposes to provide affordable housing on a site different from the proposed project site and outside the community planning area may be approved or conditionally approved only if the decision maker makes the following supplemental findings in addition to the findings in Section 142.1304(d) [*that section requires four findings prerequisite to a variance or reduction in requirements: that there are special circumstances unique to the development that justify the granting of a variance, that the development is not feasible without the modification, that a "substantial financial hardship" would occur were the modification not granted, and that no alternative means of compliance are available that would be more effective in attaining the purposes of the ordinance than the modifications requested*]:

(1) The portion of the proposed development outside of the community planning area will assist in meeting the goal of providing economically balanced communities; and

(2) The portion of the proposed development outside of the community planning area will assist in meeting the goal of providing transit oriented development.

City of San Diego, Cal., Mun. Code § 142.1304 (2008)

Boulder likewise generally requires on-site construction of inclusionary units, but it gives the city manager discretion to allow off-site compliance (assignment of such discretion in a North Carolina ordinance would need to comply with North Carolina law).

(a) ON-SITE AND OFF-SITE INCLUSIONARY ZONING REQUIREMENTS

Except as otherwise provided in this chapter ... the developer must construct a minimum of one-half of the required permanently affordable units on-site.

(b) VARIANCE TO ON-SITE CONSTRUCTION REQUIREMENT

The city manager is authorized to enter into agreements to allow a greater percentage of the required permanently affordable unit obligation to be satisfied off-site if the city manager finds:

(1) Securing such off-site units will accomplish additional benefits for the city consistent with the purposes of this chapter; or

(2) If zoning, environmental, or other legal restrictions make a particular level of on-site compliance unfeasible.

City of Boulder, Colo., Rev. Code § 9-13-6 (2009)

In-Lieu Payments

Some inclusionary zoning ordinances allow developers, under certain circumstances, to make cash payments to the local housing authority or an authorized nonprofit instead of building the affordable units. These payments, often called payments-in-lieu, buyout options, cash-in-lieu, or sometimes fees-in-lieu, are generally designed to obtain the same value for the locality that would have been realized from production of on-site inclusionary units. Typically, the amount of the payment-in-lieu is calculated by reference to the cost to the developer or to the local government to create equivalent units, or by reference to the difference in cost between a market-rate unit and an affordable unit.[18]

Some municipalities that allow payments-in-lieu establish a housing trust fund for the collection and administration of in-lieu funds. These trust funds support a number of functions, including purchase, development, and renovation of affordable housing units. The funds also provide support for programs that serve residents.

EXAMPLES

Davidson uses a formula to calculate its in-lieu fee. Note that the payment-in-lieu provision also requires that funds received by the town be set aside, so that the fee is clearly a substitute for provision of housing and not a source of revenue for the town's general fund.

> D. Payment in Lieu (PIL): Where permitted by this ordinance, the applicant may make a cash payment in lieu of providing some or all of the required affordable housing units. The Town shall establish the in-lieu per-unit cash payment on written recommendation of the Town Manager and adopt it as part of the Town's fee schedule. The per unit amount shall be based on the sales price of an affordable housing unit which is affordable to a household of four whose income does not exceed fifty percent (50%) of the Area Median Income (AMI), as published by the Department of Housing and Urban Development (HUD). At least once every three years, the Town Board shall, with the written recommendation of the Town Manager, review the per unit payment and, if necessary, amend the fees.
>
> E. Town Reservation of Funds: The Town shall receive payments in lieu and place them in a separate fund that shall be used solely and exclusively for affordable housing activities including the acquisition of land for, or the construction and marketing of, affordable dwelling units. These funds shall not be commingled with the Town's General Fund.
>
> TOWN OF DAVIDSON, N.C., PLANNING ORDINANCE § 6.3.2 (2009)

Boulder's land use code establishes a set fee for each affordable unit.

> 9-13-5 Cash-In-Lieu Equivalent for a Single Permanently Affordable Unit.

(a) Cash-In-Lieu Equivalent: Whenever this chapter permits a cash-in-lieu contribution as an alternative to the provision of a single permanently affordable unit, the cash-in-lieu contribution shall be as follows:

(1) Detached Dwelling Units: For each unrestricted detached dwelling unit, the cash-in-lieu contribution for the calendar year of 2000 shall be the lesser of $13,200.00 or $55.00 multiplied by twenty percent of the total floor area of the unrestricted unit. The cash-in-lieu contribution will be adjusted annually as set forth in subsection (c) of this section.

(2) Attached Dwelling Units: For each unrestricted attached dwelling unit, the cash-in-lieu contribution for the calendar year of 2000 shall be the lesser of $12,000.00 or $50.00 multiplied by twenty percent of the total floor area of the unrestricted unit. The cash-in-lieu contribution will be adjusted annually as set forth in subsection (c) of this section.

. . .

(c) Annual Escalator: The city manager is authorized to adjust the cash-in-lieu contribution on an annual basis to reflect changes in the median sale price for detached and attached housing, using information provided by Boulder County Assessor records for the City of Boulder.

CITY OF BOULDER, COLO., REV. CODE § 9-13-5 (2009)

Note that Boulder also provides for an affordable housing fund to administer the in-lieu contributions, and authorized expenditures of the fund include the management and maintenance of affordable housing.

(d) Affordable Housing Fund Established: The city manager shall establish an affordable housing fund for the receipt and management of permanently affordable unit cash-in-lieu financial contributions. Monies received into that fund shall be utilized solely for the construction, purchase, and maintenance of affordable housing and for the costs of administering programs consistent with the purposes of this chapter.

CITY OF BOULDER, COLO., REV. CODE § 9-13-5 (2009)

San Diego calculates its in-lieu fees based on the gross floor area of all units in the development.

> (b) The amount of the in lieu fee shall be the sum of the applicable per square foot charge multiplied by the aggregate *gross floor area* of all of the units within the *development*.
>
> (e) The amount of the in lieu fees shall be adjusted by San Diego Housing Commission, annually, commencing with the fourth year after the initial adoption of this Division, based upon 50% of the difference between the median cost of housing and housing price affordable to the median household.
>
> CITY OF SAN DIEGO, CAL., MUN. CODE § 142.1310 (2008)

Land Donation

In lieu of on-site construction, several ordinances allow a developer to donate land equivalent in value to the affordable housing units that would have been provided through on-site construction.

EXAMPLES

An earlier version of Davidson's planning ordinance required that all affordable housing units be built on-site or that developed lots on the same site be donated to the town's designee.

> 6.3.1 Options for Provision of Affordable Housing
>
> For applications with eight or more dwelling units, the applicant shall comply with either subsection (a) or (b) below . . .
>
> (a) Construct affordable dwelling units for sale or rent within the proposed development . . .
>
> (b) Convey developed lots within the development to a town affordable housing agency, to be determined by the Town, that will assume responsibility for conveyance and maintenance of dwelling units constructed on these lots.
>
> TOWN OF DAVIDSON, N.C., PLANNING ORDINANCE § 6.3.1 (2003)

Boulder seeks to ensure that donated land is of equivalent or greater value than what would have been obtained through on-site compliance.

(2) Land Dedication: To the extent permitted by this chapter, permanently affordable unit obligations may be satisfied by dedication of land in-lieu of providing affordable housing on-site. Land dedicated to the city or its designee shall be located in the City of Boulder. The value of land to be dedicated in satisfaction of this alternative means of compliance shall be determined, at the cost of the developer, by an independent appraiser, who shall be selected from a list of certified appraisers provided by the city, or by such alternative means of valuation as to which a developer and the city may agree. The land dedication requirement may be satisfied by:

    (A) Land at Equivalent Value: Conveying land to the city or its designee that is of equivalent value to the cash-in-lieu contribution that would be required [under Boulder's cash-in-lieu provisions], plus an additional fifty percent, to cover costs associated with holding, developing, improving, or conveying such land; or

    (B) Land to Construct Equivalent Units: Conveying land to the city or its designee that is of equivalent value (as of the date of the conveyance) to that land upon which required units would otherwise have been constructed (upon completion of construction). Land so deeded must be zoned such as to allow construction of at least that number of units for which the obligation of construction is being satisfied by the dedication of the land.

    (C) Dedication of Existing Units: To the extent permitted by this chapter, permanently affordable unit obligations may be satisfied by restricting existing dwelling units which are approved by the city as suitable affordable housing dwelling units through covenants, contractual arrangements, or resale restrictions . . . . Off-site units shall be located within the City of Boulder. The restriction of such existing units must result in the creation of units that are of equivalent value, quality, and size of the permanently affordable units which would have been constructed on-site if this alternative had not been utilized. Where a proposed development consists of ownership units, units created under this Section shall be ownership units. The value of dwelling units created pursuant to this Section as a way of meeting the permanently affordable unit requirement shall be determined, at the expense of the developer, by an appraiser who shall be selected by the developer from a list of certified appraisers provided by the city or by such alternative means of valuation as to which a developer and the city may agree.

CITY OF BOULDER, COLO., REV. CODE § 9-13-6(c) (2009)

The ordinance establishing and regulating the Santa Fe Homes Program (SFHP) allows developers to apply for any one of off-site construction, payment-in-lieu, or land donation as an alternative means of compliance for small projects and in cases of hardship (Santa Fe's definition of extreme hardship is provided in the earlier section on hardship clauses).

A. One of the goals and purposes of the SFHP is to foster economic integration by requiring that developers provide required SFHP units and manufactured home lots on the property proposed for development. However, it is recognized that at times this approach may not be feasible for a variety of reasons. In this event, the applicant may seek permission from the governing body to comply with the SFHP through any one or combination of the following alternative means acceptable to the city in its sole discretion: off-site construction, cash payment in lieu of constructing or creating the required SFHP units or manufactured home lots or dedication of land suitable for construction or creation of inclusionary units of equivalent or greater value than would be required for onsite construction.

B. The governing body may approve an alternate means of compliance for the following provided that any approval must be based on a finding that the purposes of this chapter would be better served by implementation of the proposed alternative(s). In determining whether the purposes of this chapter would be better served under the proposed alternative, the city shall consider all of the factors listed in [paragraph C below].

    (1) SFHP projects of eleven (11) units or more, provided that the project meets the definition of extreme hardship;

    (2) SFHP projects of ten (10) units or fewer. . . .

C. In determining whether the purposes of this chapter would be better served under the proposed alternative, the city shall consider all of the following:

    (1) Whether implementation of an alternative would overly concentrate SFHP units within any specific area and if so must reject the alternative unless the undesirable concentration of the SFHP units is offset by other identified benefits that flow from implementation of the alternative in issue; and,

    (2) The extent to which other factors affect the feasibility of prompt construction of the SFHP units on the property,

> such as costs and delays, the need for appraisal, site
> design, zoning, infrastructure, clear title, grading and
> environmental review; and,
>
> (3) The potential of leveraging funds for other needed
> affordable housing programs described in the city's
> housing plans.
>
> SANTA FE, N.M., CITY CODE § 26-1.33 (2009)

Notes

1. Nollan v. Cal. Coastal Comm'n, 483 U.S. 825 (1987); Dolan v. City of Tigard, 512 U.S. 374 (1994). These dedications of property are called exactions. See "Takings" in the Legal Appendix for a more complete discussion of exactions.

2. N.C. GEN. STAT. (hereinafter G.S.) § 160A-382. See also "Takings" in the Legal Appendix.

3. *See* General Motors Corp. v. Romein, 503 U.S. 181, 191 (1992) ("Retroactive legislation presents problems of unfairness that are more serious than those posed by prospective legislation, because it can deprive citizens of legitimate expectations and upset settled transactions. For this reason, '[t]he retroactive aspects of [economic] legislation, as well as the prospective aspects, must meet the test of due process': a legitimate legislative purpose furthered by rational means." (quoting Pension Benefit Guar. Corp. v. R.A. Gray & Co., 467 U.S. 717 (1984))).

4. *See* DAVID W. OWENS, LAND USE LAW IN NORTH CAROLINA 147 (UNC School of Government 2006) ("To establish a common law vested right in North Carolina, the landowner or the developer must have made substantial expenditures in good faith reliance on a valid government approval, with resulting detriment if he or she is required to comply with the newly adopted requirements. Each aspect of this test must be met in order for a vested right to be established.").

5. *See* Penn Central Transp. Co. v. New York City, 438 U.S. 104, 124 (1978) (establishing "investment-backed expectations" as one part of the three-pronged test for regulatory takings).

6. Rules adopted by the North Carolina Environmental Management Commission illustrate such a restatement:

> Existing development . . . shall be defined as those projects that are built
> or those projects that at a minimum have established a vested right under
> North Carolina zoning law as of the effective date of the local government
> water supply ordinance . . . based on at least one of the following criteria:

(a) substantial expenditures of resources (time, labor, money) based on a good faith reliance upon having received a valid local government approval to proceed with the project, or

(b) having an outstanding valid building permit . . . , or

(c) having an approved site specific or phased development plan . . . .

15A N.C. Admin. Code 2B § .0202(29) (2009)

For a fuller discussion of vested rights and the example provided here, see Owens, note 4 above, at 156.

7. *See* Lucas v. S.C. Coastal Council, 505 U.S. 1003, 1019 (1992). See also "Takings" in the Legal Appendix.

8. *See* Home Builders Ass'n of N. Cal. v. City of Napa, 90 Cal. App. 4th 188, 194 (2001) ("More critically, the ordinance permits a developer to appeal for a reduction, adjustment, or complete waiver of the ordinance's requirements. Since City has the ability to waive the requirements imposed by the ordinance, the ordinance cannot and does not, on its face, result in a taking."). See also "Takings" in the Legal Appendix.

9. *See* G.S. 153A-345 (counties) and G.S. 160A-388 (cities). *See also* Owens, note 4 above, at 129–35.

10. Cecily T. Talbert and Nadia L. Costa, *Current Issues in Inclusionary Zoning*, 37 Urb. Law. 513, 513 ("Housing is inseparably linked to economic and social opportunity. The level of access to quality employment, education, and social support systems, as well as the availability of a wide range of services and amenities are, in significant part, determined by where one lives."); *see also* Business and Professional People for the Public Interest, Opening the Door to Inclusionary Zoning 17 (2003) ("To create economically integrated neighborhoods, affordable housing must be built throughout the market rate development. This integration is achieved by requiring affordable units to be constructed on the same site as the market rate units. In addition, requiring the affordable units to be constructed on-site and throughout each phase of development prevents affordable housing from being clustered and prevents income-based concentration within a community.").

11. See "Takings" in the Legal Appendix.

12. *See* Nollan v. Cal. Coastal Comm'n, 483 U.S. 825 (1987); Dolan v. City of Tigard, 512 U.S. 374, 391 (1994) ("No precise mathematical calculation is required, but the city must make some sort of individualized determination that the required dedication is related both in nature and extent to the impact of the proposed development").

13. *See* Batch v. Town of Chapel Hill, 92 N.C. App. 601, 616, 376 S.E.2d 22, 31 (1989), *rev'd on other grounds,* 326 N.C. 1, 387 S.E.2d 655 (1990) (deciding that an exaction must bear "a rational nexus to the needs created by, and benefits conferred upon, the subdivision") (quoting Longridge Builders, Inc. v. Planning Bd., 245 A.2d 336, 337 (N.J. 1968)). Note that *Batch* was decided before landmark federal cases in the exactions area, such as *Dolan* and City of Monterey v. Del Monte Dunes at Monterey, Ltd., 526 U.S. 687 (1999) (clarifying that *Nollan* and *Dolan* analysis is applicable only to exactions, not to ordinances generally), so it is unclear what impact *Dolan* and later federal court decisions may have on the way North Carolina courts interpret this test.

14. Two other possible legal challenges, while unlikely to succeed if raised, are addressed by offering alternatives to on-site compliance. First, offering alternatives in a mandatory inclusionary zoning ordinance may prove helpful in overcoming a takings challenge. For example, even if an ordinance appears not to effect a taking because it does not deprive an owner of *all* economic use of property as required by *Lucas*, an inflexible ordinance may indicate that the "character" of the ordinance deserves further scrutiny as a regulatory taking under *Penn Central*. For additional discussion of regulatory takings, see "Takings" in the Legal Appendix. Second, alternative compliance options may eliminate any claim that an owner's due process rights have been violated. *See* Deborah Collins and Michael Rawson, *Avoiding Constitutional Challenges to Inclusionary Zoning, in* 3 NATIONAL HOUSING CONFERENCE AFFORDABLE HOUSING POLICY REVIEW: INCLUSIONARY ZONING: THE CALIFORNIA EXPERIENCE 32, 35–36 (2004), *available at* www.nhc.org/media/documents/IZ_CA_experiencet.pdf; Home Builders Ass'n of N. Cal. v. City of Napa, 90 Cal. App. 4th 188, 199 (2001) (". . . City's ordinance includes a clause that allows city officials to reduce, modify or waive the requirements contained in the ordinance . . . Since City has the authority to completely waive a developer's obligations, a facial challenge under the due process clause must necessarily fail.").

15. G.S. 160A-382(a) and 153A-342(a). *See also* OWENS, note 4 above, at 95–98. See also "Takings" in the Legal Appendix.

16. In North Carolina, the authority to require dedications of land or fees is part of a local government's subdivision power. See "Local Government Authority to Enact Inclusionary Zoning in North Carolina" in the Legal Appendix.

17. *Id.*

18. Ordinances containing an in-lieu payment option, even as a voluntary option for compliance, may receive heightened scrutiny in North Carolina. *See* Union Land Owners Ass'n v. County of Union, ___ N.C. App. ___, 689 S.E.2d 504 (2009) (striking down voluntary payment compliance option for adequate school facilities ordinance as *ultra vires* attempt to circumvent *Durham Land Owners Ass'n v. County of Durham*, 177 N.C.App. 629, 630 S.E.2d 200, *discretionary review denied*, 360 N.C. 532, 633 S.E.2d 678 (2006) (invalidating school impact fee as *ultra vires*)). However, the cited cases dealt with funds for school construction, which are arguably distinguishable from inclusionary zoning. For a discussion of distinctions between inclusionary zoning and the facts in *Union Land Owners*, see "Local Government Authority to Enact Inclusionary Zoning in North Carolina" in the Legal Appendix.

6

Developer Compliance Considerations

A number of inclusionary zoning ordinances regulate the manner in which a developer provides inclusionary set-aside units. These considerations typically encompass such matters as the timing of delivery of inclusionary units compared with market-rate units, the appearance and location of those units within a development, and the agreements and laws that regulate the provision of inclusionary units. These issues are addressed in detail below. As a general matter, mechanisms for enforcing these inclusionary requirements are no different than those typically available under state law for enforcement of other zoning and building laws. North Carolina local governments should consult with a local government or land use attorney to determine what remedies are presently available and appropriate under North Carolina law.[1]

Concurrent Construction of Inclusionary and Market-Rate Units

In order to ensure that affordable housing units constructed pursuant to an inclusionary zoning program are completed concurrently with market-rate units, many inclusionary ordinances have specific completion requirements. A developer may be required to produce a portion of the affordable units at each of several stages of construction of market rate units (known as "phasing"), or completion of all inclusionary units may be required prior to completion of the development and issuance of occupancy permits.[2]

The purpose of these concurrency requirements is to ensure that a developer remains committed to building all of the required affordable units.[3] Even when local governments utilize development agreements and deed restrictions to enforce inclusionary requirements,[4] some still have difficulty monitoring the construction of affordable units in the absence of concurrent or simultaneous production requirements.[5]

EXAMPLES

Manteo's ordinance requires an explicit plan for the phasing of development to integrate market-rate and affordable housing.

> *Phasing of construction.* The inclusionary housing plan and the development agreement shall include a phasing plan that provides for the timely and integrated development of the affordable housing units or lots as the covered development project is built out. The phasing plan shall provide for the development of the affordable housing units or lots concurrently with the market rate units or lots. Building permits shall be issued for the covered development project based upon the phasing plan. The phasing plan may be adjusted by the town when necessary in order to account for the different financing and funding environments, economies of scale, and infrastructure needs applicable to development of the market rate and the affordable housing units. The phasing plan shall be approved by the town Planning and Zoning Board prior to the issuance of any building permit.
>
> Town of Manteo, N.C., Zoning Code § 11-8(b) (2009)

Burlington mandates that compliance with the city's inclusionary zoning ordinance be certified by the city's housing trust fund before *any* certificate of occupancy is granted.

> Notwithstanding any other provision of this ordinance, no certificate of occupancy for a project covered by this chapter shall be granted unless and until a Certificate of Inclusionary Housing Compliance has been issued by the Manager of the city's Housing Trust Fund.
>
> City of Burlington, Vt., Comprehensive Development Ordinance § 9.1.7 (2009)

In addition, Burlington's ordinance requires that affordable units be made available at the same pace as market-rate units, and it does not allow the last certificates of occupancy to be issued until all the affordable housing units have been built.

> Inclusionary units shall be made available for occupancy on approximately the same schedule as a covered project's market units, except that certificates of occupancy for the last ten percent (10%) of the market units shall be withheld until certificates of occupancy have been issued for all of the inclusionary units; except that with respect to covered projects to be constructed in phases, certificates of occupancy may be issued on a phased basis consistent with the conditions of approval set forth by the DRB [Development Review Board] in Section 9.1.18 [regarding review of proposals for phasing].
>
> CITY OF BURLINGTON, VT., COMPREHENSIVE DEVELOPMENT ORDINANCE § 9.1.19 (2009)

Integration of Inclusionary Units within a Development

Many inclusionary zoning ordinances require affordable units to be integrated as seamlessly as possible into the rest of the development. Several characteristics are typically regulated to achieve this purpose.

Some ordinances require that affordable units be of a certain minimum square footage (greater than the housing code's minimum); that they be of similar size to comparable market-rate units; that they have an exterior finish that is substantially similar to market-rate units; or that the buildings be of similar mass. Energy efficiency may also be regulated. Exceptions are sometimes permitted by ordinance in particularly desirable locations, such as waterfront lots. Depending on how detailed the design and integration standards are, some additional review of architectural, development, management, or service plans may be required to ensure that the affordable units meet the requirements.

A number of inclusionary zoning ordinances also require that affordable units not be isolated from the rest of the development, or that they be interspersed with market rate units rather than clustered together and segregated from the market-rate units.

Requiring inclusionary set-aside units to appear similar in size and appearance to market-rate units avoids stigmatization of the residents in the affordable units and eases fears that affordable units will drive down the value of market-rate housing. Additionally, inclusionary zoning proponents have suggested that integration may help minimize "not-in-my-back-yard" (NIMBY) sentiment that might otherwise surface.[6]

EXAMPLES

Manteo explicitly requires that affordable units be visually and spatially integrated but makes an exception for waterfront lots.

> *Location of affordable housing units.* Affordable housing units or lots shall not be segregated and should be interspersed among the market rate units throughout the covered development and the locations shall be approved by the town planner.
>
> This requirement shall not require a developer to construct dwelling units on waterfront lots provided that other alternatives are available and provided that they still maintain visual and spatial integration. In condo developments, where the first floor is retail under residential and is sold as part of a single condominium, the affordable units may be in a separate building provided that the building is visually similar and not visually or spatially set aside.
>
> TOWN OF MANTEO, N.C., ZONING CODE § 11-8(a) (2009)

Carrboro likewise requires spatial integration, but it does not further define a key term, "unduly isolated or segregated."

> Affordable housing units or lots constructed or created in accordance with this section shall not be unduly isolated or segregated from other dwellings or lots that do not satisfy the "affordability" criteria set forth in this section.
>
> CARRBORO, N.C., TOWN CODE § 15-182.4(f) (2009)

Davidson requires that affordable units be functionally equivalent to market rate units, and then defines what it means by "functionally equivalent."

Home Sweet Homes

The two homes pictured here look like identical pricey properties. But the one shown at left actually contains four $125,000 town houses; the single-family home on the right that it mirrors sells for $840,000-plus.

Four-unit floor plan

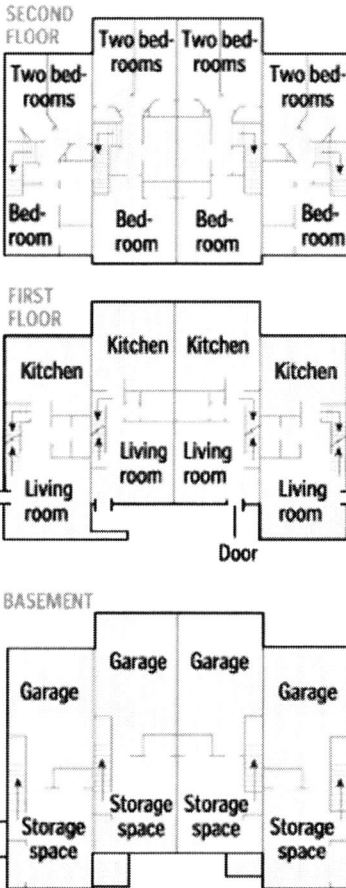

SECOND FLOOR

| Two bed-rooms | Two bed-rooms | Two bed-rooms | Two bed-rooms |
| Bed-room | Bed-room | Bed-room | Bed-room |

FIRST FLOOR

| Kitchen | Kitchen | Kitchen | Kitchen |
| Living room | Living room | Living room | Living room |

Door

BASEMENT

| Garage | Garage | Garage | Garage |
| Storage space | Storage space | Storage space | Storage space |

Single-family floor plan

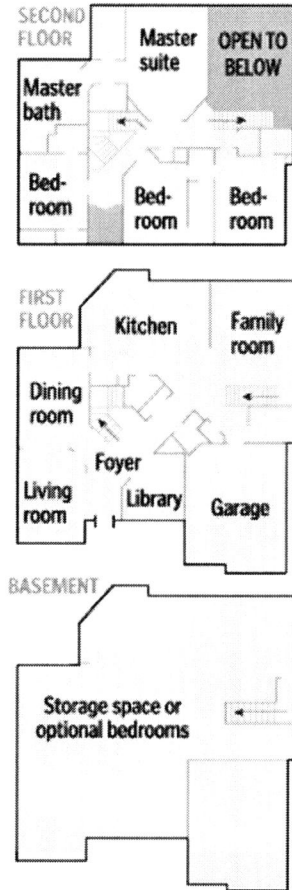

SECOND FLOOR

Master suite	OPEN TO BELOW
Master bath	
Bed-room	Bed-room	Bed-room

FIRST FLOOR

Kitchen	Family room
Dining room	
Foyer	
Living room	Library	Garage

BASEMENT

Storage space or optional bedrooms

SOURCE: Custom Design Concepts Architecture

PHOTOGRAPHS BY PETER WHORISKEY—THE WASHINGTON POST

A. Minimum Standards for Affordable Units
1. Functionally Equivalent: Affordable units shall be "functionally equivalent" to market rate units. This means that when features are included in market rate units, such as kitchen cabinets, countertops, dishwasher, etc., then equivalent features are included in the permanently affordable units. This does not mean that the features need to be identical. The Town will consider variations that result in an equivalent livability outcome.

TOWN OF DAVIDSON, N.C., PLANNING ORDINANCE § 6.3.5 (2008)

Fairfax County applies a set of design specifications to all building plans for affordable dwelling units.[7] In addition to the design specifications, Fairfax County has also developed a "Great House" credit to achieve integration of affordable housing with market-rate housing.[8] It allows sale prices for affordable dwelling units, normally based on cost, to be increased if several affordable units are built to look like a (much larger) market-rate home.[9] This ordinance also allows developers to construct higher-quality affordable units than required by the guidelines, and part of the additional cost may go into the sale price of the unit.

Any applicant or owner may voluntarily construct affordable dwelling units to a standard in excess of such specifications, but only fifty (50) percent of any added cost for exterior architectural compatibility upgrades (such as brick facade, shutters, bay windows, etc.) and additional landscaping on the affordable dwelling unit lot shall be included within recoverable costs, up to a maximum of two (2) percent of the sales price of the affordable dwelling unit, with the allowance for additional landscaping not to exceed one-half (1/2) of the above-noted two (2) percent maximum.

COUNTY OF FAIRFAX, VA., ZONING ORDINANCE § 2-809(1) (2009)

Burlington's ordinance requires affordable units to be similar to market rate units in a number of ways, including bedroom mix, exterior appearance, and energy efficiency. It also requires a minimum square footage for each unit size. If size requirements are to be a part of a community's inclusionary zoning ordinance, drafters should consider what minimum unit sizes would be most appropriate for housing in their community.

All covered projects must comply with the requirements set forth below.

    (a) In order to assure an adequate distribution of inclusionary units by household size, the bedroom mix of inclusionary units in any project shall be in the same ratio as the bedroom mix of the non-inclusionary units of the project;

    (b) Inclusionary units may differ from the market units in a covered project with regard to interior amenities and gross floor area, provided that:

        1. These differences, excluding differences related to size differentials, are not apparent in the general exterior appearance of the project's units; and

        2. These differences do not include insulation, windows, heating systems, and other improvements related to the energy efficiency of the project's units; and

    (c) The gross floor area of the inclusionary units is not less than the following minimum requirements, unless waived by the DRB [Development Review Board, a quasi-judicial body that reviews development proposals, issues permits and variances, and hears appeals] using the following criteria:

        1. All of the units being provided with a specific bedroom count are smaller than the standards outlined below;

        2. More than the required number of inclusionary units are provided on site, not all shall be subject to bedroom mix and size requirement; or,

        3. The units have an efficient floor plan (meaning that less than 5% of the square footage is devoted to circulation) and the bedroom size(s) is a minimum of 144sf or 12'x12'.

One bedroom .... 750 square feet
Two bedroom...1,000 square feet
Three bedroom..1,100 square feet
Four bedroom ....1,250 square feet

City of Burlington, Vt., Comprehensive Development Ordinance § 9.1.15 (2009)

Boulder bases its unit size requirements on the size of market-rate units in the development.

MINIMUM SIZES FOR PERMANENTLY AFFORDABLE UNITS
The minimum size for permanently affordable units shall be as follows:
  (1) The average floor area of the detached permanently
      affordable units in a development shall be a minimum
      of forty-eight percent of the average floor area of all the
      non-permanently affordable units which are part of the
      same development up to a maximum average size of
      1,200 square feet of floor area.
  (2) The average floor area of the attached permanently
      affordable units in a development shall be a minimum of
      eighty percent of the average floor area of all the non-
      permanently affordable units which are part of the same
      development up to a maximum average size of 1,200
      square feet of floor area.

CITY OF BOULDER, COLO., REV. CODE § 9-13-4(c) (2009)

Napa requires the exterior of all units to be similar, although if Napa's language is followed, a municipality may want to include some design review or further guidance as to how appearance should be comparable. Since North Carolina law limits the extent to which local governments can delegate their authority, such design review may need to be conducted by a quasi-judicial body provided with adequate standards to guide its judgment.[10]

Affordable units shall be comparable in number of bedrooms, exterior appearance and overall quality of construction to market rate units in the same residential project. Subject to the approval of the planning director and housing director, square footage of affordable units and interior features in affordable units may not be the same as or equivalent to those in market rate units in the same residential project, so long as they are of good quality and are consistent with contemporary standards for new housing. Affordable units shall be dispersed throughout the residential project, or, subject to the approval of the planning director and housing director, may be clustered within the residential project when this furthers affordable housing opportunities.

CITY OF NAPA, CAL., MUN. CODE § 15.94.050(I) (2005)

Consistent Tenancy or Manner of Ownership

Some ordinances require affordable units to mirror the tenancy of the larger development; in other words, rental developments must offer affordable rental units, and for-sale developments must offer affordable for-sale units. This potentially raises a legal concern in North Carolina, because North Carolina courts have struck down local government zoning that purports to regulate the manner of ownership of property (either as for-sale or for-rent).[11] These cases apply only to the regulations themselves; therefore, as long as no mandate appears in the zoning ordinance, it may still be possible to achieve an equivalent result by contractual agreement with the owner or developer.[12] Regardless, caution should be exercised when attempting to control the manner of ownership of property.

EXAMPLE

Davidson has avoided this particular issue entirely by requiring only that affordable units be affordable to qualified households. The ordinance does not specify what form of ownership must be utilized. If the unit is offered for sale, it must be sold at the required affordable sale price; if rented, it must be offered to eligible households at an affordable rent. Because the Davidson ordinance allows for affordable units to be either sold or rented, it cannot be viewed as impermissibly regulating manner of ownership.

> General Requirement. Except as otherwise provided, 12.5% of the total number of residential units within any development shall be affordable housing units and shall be located on the site of the development.
>
> TOWN OF DAVIDSON, N.C., PLANNING ORDINANCE § 6.3.2.B.1 (2008)

Development Plans and Agreements

Many subsidized housing programs, including inclusionary zoning programs, require the developer to enter into an agreement with the local government regarding construction and management of affordable housing units. In North Carolina, cities and counties possess authority to enter into development agreements in compliance with state law.[13]

Such agreements typically cover the following:

- The relative roles and responsibilities of the developer, the local government, and any third parties (such as management entities)[14]
- Any subsidies received by the developer[15]
- The anticipated phasing and timing of construction of affordable units with market-rate units[16]
- Affordability restrictions to be applied to units[17]
- Marketing of affordable units[18]
- Qualification of buyers or renters of affordable units[19]
- Management of the affordable units on resale or re-rental[20]
- Any other specifics necessary to ensure that the units are maintained as affordable

In North Carolina, such an agreement serves another purpose. It keeps the affordability restrictions from running afoul of North Carolina's rent control statute, which provides an exception for rent control exercised through "agreements with private persons" to regulate subsidized rental housing.[21]

EXAMPLES

Manteo requires that a development agreement and associated inclusionary housing plan be in place before a building permit may be issued.

> Prior to issuance of a building permit for any covered development, the applicant shall have entered into a development agreement with the town regarding the specific requirements and restrictions regarding affordable housing and the covered development. The applicant shall execute any and all documents deemed necessary by the town, including without limitation, restrictive covenants and other related instruments, to ensure the continued affordability of the affordable housing units or lots in accordance with this chapter. The development agreement shall set forth the commitments and obligations of the town and the applicant and shall incorporate, among other things, the inclusionary housing plan, all to be recorded in the Dare County Register of Deeds.
>
> TOWN OF MANTEO, N.C., ZONING CODE § 11-6 (2009)

The "inclusionary housing plan" mentioned in the provision above is defined as follows, including a description of the number, location, pricing, and phasing of each unit.

> (b) *Inclusionary housing plan.* As part of the approval of a covered development project, the applicant shall present to the town an inclusionary housing plan that outlines and specifies the covered development's compliance with each of the applicable requirements of this ordinance and regulations adopted by the Board of Commissioners. The plan shall be subject to approval by the town and shall be incorporated into the development agreement between the applicant and the town and recorded in the Dare County Register of Deeds. The plan shall specifically contain, at a minimum, the following information regarding the covered development:
> (1) A general description of the development.
> (2) The total number of market rate units or lots and affordable units or lots in the development.
> (3) The location within any multiple-family residential structure and any single-family residential development of each market rate unit or lot and each affordable unit or lot.
> (4) The pricing for each affordable housing unit or lot. The pricing of each unit or lot shall be determined at time of approval. At time of sale this price may be adjusted if there has been a change in the median income or a change in the formulas used in this ordinance.
> (5) The phasing for each market rate unit and each affordable unit.
>
> Town of Manteo, N.C., Zoning Code § 11-4 (2009)

Montgomery County requires a detailed development agreement for all projects that will provide affordable housing units.

> Requirements of the Agreement to Build Moderately Priced Dwelling Units [MPDU].
> (a) Once the Planning Board has set the MPDU requirements for the subdivision, an applicant must enter into a written Agreement to Build Moderately Priced Dwelling Units with the Department in a form approved by the Department. This Agreement must be executed

before any building permits within the subdivision may be issued by
the Department of Permitting Services (DPS). The Agreement must
contain at least the following information:

(1) The name of the subdivision, the marketing name if
different than the subdivision, the apartment or condominium name, when applicable. A copy of the approved
preliminary plan or the record plat must be provided with
the agreement.

(2) A plan for the staging of construction of all dwelling units
that is consistent with [the MPDU program requirements]
and any approved applicable land use, subdivision, or site
plan.

(3) A copy of the applicable covenants, either rental or sales
covenants.

(4) The Agreement must identify all land which is owned
by or under contract of sale to the applicant, or, will be
available, or is being processed for development and individually or collectively will be subject to [MPDU program
requirements]. For subsequent MPDU construction agreements, it will be necessary only to update this statement.

(b) The Department must determine that the Agreement meets the
[MPDU program requirements] and these regulations. Any revisions to
the Agreement must be requested in writing from the developer, and
approved in writing by the Director.

(c) A copy of the executed Agreement must be submitted to DPS
with the first building permits application in the subdivision. DPS must
not issue building permits in a subdivision having an MPDU requirement unless those units are included in the signed Agreement.

Montgomery County, Md., Code Regs. (COMCOR) § 25A.00.02.03.1 (2003)

Resolving Conflicts with Other Local Regulations

Regardless of the community, inclusionary zoning requirements will not be
the only development controls in force. For instance, many communities
impose minimum lot size requirements, setback minimums, or height restrictions that may need to be adjusted to allow for affordable units. Others may
have open space or tree preservation ordinances that could cause conflicts
with some inclusionary zoning requirements or incentives.

Consequently, there may be areas of local regulation where restrictions need to be prioritized. For instance, if the program will include reductions in setback requirements or density bonuses, should these come before or after any tree preservation or open space set-asides? Most inclusionary zoning ordinances deal with these conflicts in one or both of the following ways:

- The ordinance anticipates the most common conflicts and addresses them directly through special exceptions or rules of priority
- The ordinance gives the local planning body discretion to handle any unforeseen conflicts in local regulation

In many jurisdictions, developers may be permitted to provide fewer affordable housing units if they would otherwise run afoul of open space or environmental restrictions. In a few others, development rules are less restrictive where affordable housing units are built.

EXAMPLES

Some of the flexibility built into Montgomery County's ordinance is designed to ensure that the density bonuses provided for in its ordinance do not cause violations of other ordinances.

(a) The Director may allow fewer or no [inclusionary units] to be built in a development with more than 20 but fewer than 50 units at one location in accordance with Section 25A-5(d)(1) if the Planning Board, in reviewing a subdivision or site plan submitted by the applicant, and based on the lot size, product type, and other elements of the plan as submitted, finds that building the required number of [inclusionary units] at that location:
> (1) Would not allow compliance with applicable environmental standards and other regulatory requirements . . .

MONTGOMERY COUNTY, MD., CODE REGS. (COMCOR) § 25A.00.02.04.6 (2003)

Carrboro, which applies an open space set-aside to new developments, reduces that set-aside where a developer agrees to construct affordable homes.

(e) Within any development that provides affordable housing units or affordable housing lots, the minimum area that must be set aside as open space . . . may be reduced by an amount equal to twice the land area consumed by all such affordable housing units or lots, except in no case may the required percentage of open space be less than 20 percent (10 percent in the [downtown mixed-use] and [highest-density residential] districts).

CARRBORO, N.C., TOWN CODE § 15-182.4 (2009)

Carrboro also allows for reduced setback requirements.

(d) The board of adjustment may issue a special exception permit . . . to allow a reduction of up to 50% in the required distances that buildings must be set back from lot boundary lines . . . provided that:

(1) The reduction may be permitted only for buildings on lots used for conforming residential purposes in residential districts, where . . . the lot is to be developed or redeveloped using the residential density bonus for affordable housing . . .

(2) In no case may the reduction allow a building to be located closer to a lot boundary line than a distance equal to one-half of the minimum building separation requirement established by the North Carolina State Building Code or allow the location of a building in such proximity to a pre-existing building as to violate the minimum building separation requirement of the North Carolina State Building Code;

(3) Reductions may be allowed under this section only for setbacks from lot boundary lines, not setbacks from street right-of-way lines.

CARRBORO, N.C., TOWN CODE § 15-92.1(d) (2009)

Notes

1. For instance, local governments may seek injunctions to compel compliance with land development regulations and remedy violations of zoning ordinances or building codes, *see* N.C. GEN. STAT. (hereinafter G.S.) §§ 153A-123(d), (e) and 160A-175 (d),(e).

See also David W. Owens, Land Use Law in North Carolina 174–78 (UNC School of Government 2006).

2. California Affordable Housing Law Project & Western Center on Law and Poverty, Inclusionary Zoning: Policy Considerations and Best Practices 8 (2002) (hereinafter IZ Best Practices).

3. Business and Professional People for the Public Interest, Opening the Door to Inclusionary Zoning 14 (2003) (hereinafter BPI).

4. For more on deed restrictions and their function in inclusionary zoning ordinances, see "Deed Restrictions, Deeds of Trust, and Ground Leases" in Chapter 7.

5. IZ Best Practices, note 2 above, at 8.

6. BPI, note 3 above, at 15–16.

7. The design specifications may be found at Fairfax County Specifications for Prototype Affordable Dwelling Units (Sept. 15, 1999), *available at* www.fairfaxcounty.gov/rha/adu/SPECS-5-2002.pdf.

8. For more on the Great House program, see generally HUD USER Regulatory Barriers Clearinghouse, Fairfax, Virginia Great House Program, www.huduser.org/rbc/search/rbcdetails.asp?DocId=461.

9. *See* Fairfax County Sales Prices for Affordable Dwelling Units § 3.5 (July 1, 2001), *available at* www.fairfaxcounty.gov/rha/adu/pricingnarrative701.pdf; Fairfax County Affordable Dwelling Unit (ADU) Program Addendum to Schedule of ADU Prototypes and Cost Allowances, ADU Price Adjustments (Nov. 15, 2007), *available at* www.fairfaxcounty.gov/rha/adu/adupriceadj.pdf.

10. *See* Owens, note 1 above, at 121–24.

11. A panel of the North Carolina Court of Appeals struck down a zoning ordinance requiring an owner of a home having a garage apartment to occupy either the main house or the garage apartment, which would have prevented the owner from renting both the house and the apartment. *See* City of Wilmington v. Hill, 189 N.C. App. 173, 657 S.E.2d 670 (2008). See also *Graham Court Associates v. Town Council of Town of Chapel Hill*, 53 N.C. App. 543, 546–47, 281 S.E.2d 418, 420 (1981), on which the *Wilmington* court relied.

12. *See* North Carolina law explicitly recognizes this practice in its rent control statute. *See* G.S. 42-14.1(2).

13. *See* Part 3A of G.S. Chapter 153A (counties) and Part 3D of G.S. Chapter 160A (cities). For a discussion of North Carolina law as it pertains to development agreements, see Owens, note 1 above, 155–156.

14. See "Managing Inclusionary Units" in Chapter 7.

15. Subsidies received by the developer may or may not include incentives provided through the inclusionary zoning program. For a thorough discussion of incentives, see Chapter 4.

16. See "Concurrent Construction of Inclusionary and Market-Rate Units," above.

17. See "Transfer Controls" in Chapter 7.

18. See "Marketing of Inclusionary Units" in Chapter 7.

19. See "Resident Eligibility and Qualification" in Chapter 7.

20. See "Managing Inclusionary Units" in Chapter 7.

21. *See* G.S. 42-14.1. The rent control statute contains an exemption for "agreements with private persons which regulate the amount of rent charged for subsidized rental properties," G.S. 42-14.1(2). A development agreement, combined with incentives for the production of affordable housing units, arguably falls under this exception. For more on the rent control issue, see "North Carolina Limitation on Rent Control" in the Legal Appendix.

7

Occupancy and Transfer Controls

Once affordable housing units are produced under an inclusionary zoning ordinance, local officials must undertake a number of tasks. Among them are the following:

- Designating an authority to manage inclusionary units, whether for rental or sale
- Establishing a system to qualify prospective buyers or tenants as eligible for affordable units
- Deciding how long inclusionary units will remain subject to affordability requirements
- Enacting measures to preserve the affordability of inclusionary units over time

Each of these tasks is discussed below.

Managing Inclusionary Units

In most of the programs surveyed for this publication, inclusionary units remain in private hands after they are built. Requiring inclusionary units to be deeded over to the local government or a nonprofit would oblige the local government to provide compensation to the developer.[1] Rather than take ownership of the units, some local governments provide management services for the owner.

Management of rental units does not have to be performed by the owner. For example, a local government may arrange for its housing authority to manage affordable rental properties, even though a private party retains ownership of the units. Some municipalities also enlist the help of nonprofits in managing affordable rental properties.[2]

There are three core areas of management:

1. Qualification and tracking of residents eligible to rent or purchase affordable units
2. Assignment of eligible residents to units (and waiting list management)
3. Property management of rental units

Item number 3, property management of rental units, may take one of the following forms:

- The units remain in private hands, but local government officials qualify tenants and monitor units to ensure that they are being rented to qualified households at the affordable rate.
- The local government or housing authority purchases the inclusionary units and manages them itself.
- The local government designates certain nonprofits as eligible purchasers and/or managers of affordable units.[3]

EXAMPLES

Davidson allows developers to enter into agreements with approved nonprofits, which then assume the developer's obligation to provide affordable housing units.[4]

> B. Contract with Approved Affordable Housing Provider. The following components will be required in the agreement between the developer and the Approved Affordable Housing Provider:
>   1. Provider to Assume Ordinance Obligations: The Approved Affordable Housing Provider agrees to assume the obligations of the developer to provide affordable housing under this ordinance.
>   2. Financial Arrangement: The terms of financial arrangement shall be disclosed to ensure that the Developer will compensate the Provider adequately for meeting those obligations including but not limited to property acquisition, unit construction, unit subsidy, marketing expenses, and homeowner education.

> 3. Penalty for Failure to Perform: Upon the determination that the Developer has failed to fulfill the agreement with the Provider, in addition to any other legal consequences, the Town has the right to deny issuance of building permits or revoke certificates of occupancy for any unoccupied units. The Planning Director for the Town may determine whether the Developer has failed to comply with this section.
>
> C. Completeness Review: Neither the affordable housing plan or the contract with an affordable housing provider shall be accepted by the Planning Director unless it contains all of the information that is necessary for the Town to determine whether or not the development, if completed as proposed, will comply with all of the requirements of this section.
>
> TOWN OF DAVIDSON, N.C., PLANNING ORDINANCE § 6.3.3 (2008)

The approved affordable housing provider can be any nonprofit, governmental, or nongovernmental agency, as long as it submits a plan detailing its involvement in the inclusionary zoning program.

> **Approved Affordable Housing Providers**
>
> Non-profit organizations, governmental agencies, or quasi-governmental agencies may be certified by the Town Board as an "Approved Affordable Housing Provider" subject to the following provisions:
>
> A. They shall be a non-profit organization under section 501(c)(3) of the US Tax Code or shall be a directly funded agency of a unit of government; and
>
> B. They shall present a plan indicating how the organization will participate in meeting the Town's affordable housing goals as stated in [the preamble to the ordinance]; and
>
> C. On an annual basis, they shall report to the Town Board their progress in meeting the plan in (b) above as well as its progress in fulfilling the obligations it has undertaken under contracts with developers under Section 6.3.3.
>
> TOWN OF DAVIDSON, N.C., PLANNING ORDINANCE § 6.3.4 (2008)

In Montgomery County, many rental moderately priced dwelling units (MPDUs) are owned by nonprofit organizations that must be qualified and licensed by the county.

Qualification and Designation of Housing Providers by the County Executive.

(a) From time to time, the Director [of the county's Department of Housing and Community Affairs] may recommend to the County Executive that certain housing development agencies and nonprofit corporations be approved to purchase MPDUs. To be eligible for such a designation, the housing provider must demonstrate its financial ability to acquire, operate, maintain and manage an MPDU satisfactorily on a long term basis. The County Executive may consider the relative needs and requirements of the housing providers and their clientele, readiness and ability of the housing provider to purchase and manage an MPDU, and the number of units previously obtained by the designated housing provider. The County Executive shall designate the housing providers approved to purchase MPDUs by Executive Order.

(b) Designated housing providers must submit a report on a bi-annual basis to the Department, or its designee, that provides the following information: number of units currently in the housing provider's program and the monthly rental rate for each unit, information concerning the tenant's gross household income, household composition, and names of employers, unit operating expenses and revenues received by the housing provider. The Director must evaluate the designated housing provider and make a recommendation to the County Executive to extend or terminate the housing provider's right to purchase MPDUs.

MONTGOMERY COUNTY, MD., CODE REGS. (COMCOR) § 25A.00.02.07.1 (2003)

Resident Eligibility and Qualification

In order to ensure that units produced by an inclusionary zoning ordinance are occupied by households in need of affordable housing, some communities require prospective residents to document their income and assets. Some ordinances also require resident training—such as first-time homebuyer education—as a prerequisite to resident qualification. This qualification process can be administered by the local government agency responsible for enforcing the provisions of the ordinance, or it can be assigned to selected nonprofit organizations.

EXAMPLES

Davidson requires that eligible households obtain a certificate of qualification stating that they meet the ordinance's requirements for eligibility. The process for matching residents with units is carried out by the owner or developer, subject to the town manager's approval. Priority is given to certain households, a feature that carries legal risks and is discussed later in this section.

> B. Affordable Units for Eligible Households Only: No person shall sell, rent, purchase, or lease an affordable unit created pursuant to this Ordinance except to eligible households and in compliance with the provisions of this Ordinance. The Town shall adopt and review, at least every three years, asset limitations.
> 1. A "certificate of qualification" must be provided to the Town of Davidson confirming that eligibility guidelines have been met.
> 2. Priority will be given to households in which the head of the household or the spouse or domestic partner is a former Davidson resident, or who works, lives or has relatives in Davidson.
> 3. A developer or owner may select a low income purchaser after completing a good faith marketing and selection process approved by the Town Manager. Upon request, the Town may provide the developer or owner of an affordable unit with a list of households certified by the Town as eligible to purchase the unit. However, a developer or property owner may select a low-income purchaser who is not on a furnished list so long as the Town can verify that eligibility guidelines have been met, as evidenced by the certificate of qualification, and that the unit is sold at an affordable price as described in this Ordinance.
>
> TOWN OF DAVIDSON, N.C., PLANNING ORDINANCE § 6.3.5.B (2008)

Montgomery County requires households that wish to rent or buy a moderately priced dwelling unit (MPDU) to demonstrate that their incomes fall within the ordinance's limits and to obtain a certificate of eligibility from the county.

(a) A person who wants to purchase or rent an MPDU must apply to the Department to be certified as eligible for participation in the program and to be placed on the eligibility list. To determine whether an individual or household meets the minimum eligibility requirements, the following information and documentation must be provided to the Department: for persons seeking rental certificates only: copies of the two most recent previously filed Federal income tax returns, the applicant's two most recent W-2 forms, copies of divorce or separation agreements (if applicable or if most recent tax return was filed as "married"), and copies of employment pay check stubs from each current employer. For persons seeking a certificate of eligibility to purchase, the applicant must also supply a credit report which is no more than thirty (30) days old. All the required information and documentation listed above must be provided for every wage earner in the household. The Department reserves the right to require certified copies of a household's IRS tax forms.

(b) Persons who do not have the required Federal tax information because they did not live in the United States at any time during the applicable time period must supply a copy of their passport and the passports of each family member indicating their dates of entry. In addition, these persons must supply evidence from the United States Internal Revenue Service verifying that they have not filed Federal income taxes in the previous one or two years, whichever is applicable.

(c) A household which includes a person who is self-employed must demonstrate that they are within the Program's income guidelines by providing evidence and documentation in a form acceptable to the Department.

. . .

(e) A household determined to be eligible is issued a non-transferable Certificate of Eligibility which contains an expiration date. The expiration date of rental certificates generally shall be twenty-four months from the date of issuance. The expiration date for certificates for sale units shall generally be the last day of the month, twelve months from the date of application. If a certificate for sale units expires prior to the next open application period, the Department may honor the certificate until the holder re-applies and is determined to be eligible. Prior to its expiration date, the Certificate of Eligibility remains valid as long as the household's income does not exceed the income limits of the MPDU program at the time the holder's mortgage loan application is submitted for underwriting by a lender or a lease for the rental of an MPDU. A certificate of eligibility may be renewed upon expiration if the certificate holder re-applies and demonstrates that the household continues to meet all eligibility requirements in effect at the time of renewal.

MONTGOMERY COUNTY , MD., CODE REGS. (COMCOR) § 25A.00.02.02.1 (2003)

Santa Fe requires prospective buyers of affordable housing units to attend a training course.

Certified means a buyer of a Santa Fe Homes Program Unit or renter of such unit whose income has been verified by the city or its agent as meeting the income limits which establish eligibility to buy or rent under the program. Buyers shall also receive a certificate verifying they have completed homebuyer training courses as part of the certification process.

SANTA FE, N.M., CITY CODE § 26-1.5 (2009)

Santa Fe also authorizes a city department to certify nonprofit organizations to perform income certifications and manage waiting lists for units produced by its Santa Fe Homes Program (SFHP).

For each development with SFHP homes or SFHP manufactured home lots for sale . . . the office of affordable housing shall designate a qualified organization(s) to provide income certifications and maintenance of waiting lists. The office of affordable housing shall establish an equitable process for selecting the organization or organizations providing these services, which process shall provide an opportunity for the developer to provide input as to the organization(s) selected. The organization and the SFHP developer shall enter into a written agreement that describes the scope of services and, if appropriate, fee structure. The SFHP developer may not terminate such agreement with the organization without the consent of the office of affordable housing. Notwithstanding those requirements, and in order to assure access to SFHP homes and manufactured home lots by all potentially qualified SFHP buyers, any other service provider operating a home-buyer training, counseling and certification program approved by the office of affordable housing may refer its clients to the selected organization for possible purchases of the SFHP homes or manufactured home lots. A SFHP developer may enter into agreements with outside entities to provide marketing or other services, which agreement shall not require approval from the office of affordable housing.

Santa Fe, N.M., City Code § 26-1.20(D) (2009)

San Diego requires certification that a prospective buyer or renter qualifies on a per-transaction basis.

The eligibility of each prospective buyer and the sales price under the restrictions set forth above shall be certified by the San Diego Housing Commission. Applicants shall submit documentation for certification to the San Diego Housing Commission for a determination of buyer eligibility prior to close of Escrow on each restricted unit.

City of San Diego, Cal., Inclusionary Affordable Hous. Implementation & Monitoring Procedures Manual 2 (revised Mar. 2008)

Preferences for Certain Populations

In addition to encouraging the provision of housing for families at particular income levels, some inclusionary zoning programs provide preferential status to certain segments of the workforce, such as local residents and public employees.

Three variations of such preferences have appeared in inclusionary zoning ordinances:

1. An occupation-related requirement; for example, that the applicant must be a public employee or an employee of a business in the jurisdiction, or that some member of the household must be employed in the jurisdiction

2. A durational residency requirement; for example, that the applicant must have lived in the municipality for a given length of time
3. A higher maximum eligible household income for certain households (usually the households of persons employed in specific occupations)

There is, however, legal risk involved with preferring certain applicants over others on some basis other than income. A principal concern is that a durational residency requirement may violate the "right to travel" pursuant to the Commerce Clause of the U.S. Constitution,[5] as well as the Privileges and Immunities Clause of the U.S. Constitution.[6] Depending on how a preference is designed, it could also potentially be a violation of the right to equal protection under the law provided by the Fourteenth Amendment.[7]

Communities attempt to address the legal issues raised by population preferences in a variety of ways, but each typically involves broadening the preference in one way or another. For instance, some programs provide a preference for households with members employed in the community in addition to a preference for households meeting a residency requirement. This approach diversifies the pool of preferred households and reduces potential disparate impacts. In any case, such preferences should be carefully tailored to avoid potential legal pitfalls, and the basis for any preference should be the subject of a specific finding (perhaps set out in a preamble to the ordinance, as discussed in Chapter 2).

The examples below illustrate the various mechanisms employed by inclusionary zoning programs to implement population preferences. No such preferences in inclusionary zoning ordinances have been tested in court, and short of the guidance provided in this section, the legal limits have not been clearly defined. Accordingly, there is no way of knowing which policies would pass legal muster if challenged. Any such preference, therefore, should be drafted in close consultation with a local government attorney.

EXAMPLES

A fairly safe approach would be to design the eligibility criteria in such a way that preferred populations are included in the eligible pool of residents but are not offered special preferences. For example, Montgomery County officials are permitted to increase the qualifying household income level for inclusionary units—an income level that applies to all potential applicants—to ensure that the starting salary of a public school teacher qualifies.

At the time the new income limits are set each year, the Department shall compare the maximum income needed to purchase for household size of one with the starting salary for a teacher (Bachelor degree) in the Montgomery County Public School System. If the Department determines that the maximum income figure under the Program would preclude the participation of a first year teacher in the school system, the Director may adjust the income limits accordingly to allow the participation of first year teachers.

MONTGOMERY COUNTY, MD., CODE REGS. (COMCOR) § 25A.00.02.02.2(e) (2003)

Along the same lines, Santa Fe's qualifying income limits are set higher for residents in certain occupations.

An eligible buyer meeting the criteria of emergency worker, first responder, teacher or related educational employees in Santa Fe County whose household income exceeds one hundred percent (100%) of area median income (AMI) but does not exceed one hundred twenty percent (120%) of AMI shall be eligible to purchase an SFHP unit in income range 4. [*i.e.*, a home available to households with incomes of 80% to 100% of AMI.]
  (1) The status of the buyer as an emergency worker or first responder shall be noted on the certificate of eligibility and shall be verified by the office of affordable housing.
  (2) The office of affordable housing shall maintain a list of occupations that meet the requirement of emergency worker, first responder or essential worker, which shall include:
    (a) Police officers;
    (b) Nurses;
    (c) Emergency medical technicians;
    (d) Firefighters;
    (e) Other health and safety workers whose services are crucial to community safety in an emergency situation; and
    (f) Teachers and related educational employees.

SANTA FE, N.M., CITY CODE § 26-1.21(E) (2009)

Dare County's ordinance defines eligible households to include a requirement that someone in the household be employed in the county.

Eligible Household: A group of individuals who occupy one housing unit on a year-round basis with a total combined adjusted gross annual income at or below the Median Family Income for Dare County; the individuals may, but are not required to be related by marriage or kinship. For purposes of this section, the income of all individuals age 18 or older residing in the housing unit shall be counted toward the total adjusted gross annual income for the eligible household, excluding income earned by any member of the household who is enrolled in good standing and pursuing a degree program at an accredited college or university. *At least 1 member of the eligible household age 18 years or older must be employed in Dare County.*

DARE COUNTY, N.C., ZONING ORDINANCE § 22-58.3(b)(2) (2008) (emphasis added)

The lottery process by which units are offered for sale in Montgomery County includes points for living and for working in the county and gives priority to those with more points.

Lottery Selection Process. After the Department has approved the Offering Agreement, eligible persons who are interested in purchasing MPDUs, other than the Commission, and designated, non-profit housing providers must be selected through a lottery process conducted by the Department in cooperation with the applicant. This process must be used to establish a lottery list of eligible certificate holders to whom the available MPDUs must be offered for sale.

    (a) The Department must notify the applicant and eligible certificate holders of the proposed offering. A lottery entry form may be included with the offering notice sent to eligible certificate holders. This form must be completed and returned to the Department by the date indicated on the form in order to be entered into the lottery drawing. At the time a household is determined to be eligible under the Program, the Department awards points according to the factors listed below:

        (1) One (1) point for each consecutive year (12 month period) the person has held a Certificate of Eligibility for

the MPDU sales program, up to a maximum of three (3) points;

(2) One (1) point for living in the County at the time of application to the lottery, for a maximum of one (1) point;

(3) One (1) point for working in the County at the time of application to the lottery, for a maximum of one (1) point; and

(4) The maximum number of points that may be assigned to an eligible certificate holder is five (5) points.

(5) Points awarded under items (2) and (3) must be revoked if the eligible certificate holder does not meet the applicable criteria at the time of the drawing.

(b) One person households may only be permitted to participate in lottery drawings for one and two bedroom units; two person households may be eligible to participate in lottery drawings for dwelling units containing up to three bedrooms. One person households may not be permitted to purchase any MPDUs with three (3) or more bedrooms or conventional townhouses with two (2) bedrooms unless the lottery list of eligible households containing two (2) or more people has been completely exhausted. The Director may waive this limitation for good cause.

(c) The lottery drawing shall commence by drawing first from among those eligible certificate holders who have been assigned the highest number of points. A lottery list of names must be developed, with the order determined by the order in which the names were drawn. The applicant must offer those eligible certificate holders highest on the list the first opportunity to purchase the available MPDUs.

MONTGOMERY COUNTY, MD., CODE REGS. (COMCOR) § 25A.00.02.06.2 (2003)

Control Period

All inclusionary zoning programs provide a control period; that is, a length of time for which the affordability controls must be maintained. Control periods vary greatly, with some as short as fifteen years[8] and others as long as ninety-nine years[9] or even in perpetuity or as long as permissible by law.[10] For those ordinances that require units to remain affordable in perpetuity, some define "in perpetuity" to mean for the life of the project, which may be further defined by a number such as fifty or ninety-nine years.[11]

While inclusionary zoning advocates tend to prefer longer control periods in order to slow the loss of inclusionary units,[12] a very long control period may not allow a property to adapt to major changes in land use in the surrounding area over time. To address the latter concern, an inclusionary ordinance can provide for a procedure by which owners of inclusionary units may petition for an early end to the control period.[13] In some communities with shorter control periods, the inclusionary zoning ordinance provides for the period to reset if an owner sells the home before the control period ends.

EXAMPLES

Manteo's ordinance aims for perpetual affordability but states that its control period will not last longer than allowed by law.

> *Sale of affordable housing units or lots.* In covered developments that contain for-sale units or lots, affordable housing units or lots shall be resold to low- and moderate-income households in perpetuity or as long as permissible by law.
>
> TOWN OF MANTEO, N.C., ZONING CODE § 11-12 (2009)

Burlington applies a ninety-nine-year control period but establishes a process by which a quasi-judicial review board may modify the duration.

> 99-Year Requirement. All inclusionary units shall remain affordable for a period of no less than ninety-nine (99) years commencing from the date of initial occupancy of the units. Where a developer can establish that regulatory or other considerations make it impossible to provide the required inclusionary units if subject to the full extent of this requirement, the development review board may modify the duration of the period of continued affordability only to the extent necessary to render the development feasible;
>
> CITY OF BURLINGTON, VT., COMPREHENSIVE DEVELOPMENT ORDINANCE § 9.1.17(a) (2009)

Transfer Controls

Inclusionary zoning ordinances typically require developers, owners, and tenants to comply with one or more transfer restrictions in order to keep the inclusionary units from being sold or leased at market rate prior to the end of the control period. The following transfer controls are typically used:

- Deed restrictions, deeds of trust, and ground leases
- Rights of first refusal when for-sale units are resold
- Equity sharing mechanisms, in which owner-occupants gain some, but not all, of the appreciation in their homes' value upon resale
- Measures to prevent the lease or sublease of inclusionary units at market rates
- Marketing requirements for unoccupied inclusionary units

Each of these is discussed below.

Deed Restrictions, Deeds of Trust, and Ground Leases

The most common method of enforcing the price of an affordable home on resale is by deed restriction. However, deed restrictions are of somewhat limited value in controlling resale prices, as participants in the closing process may overlook the deed restrictions when the property is sold. This is even more likely to occur when the deed restriction does not contain an enforceable requirement that notice of the sale be provided to the organization charged with managing inclusionary units.

To address these concerns, a number of inclusionary zoning programs require the recording of a deed of trust or mortgage lien on the property. The advantages of a deed of trust are that it must typically be released prior to any sale, and a violation of a deed of trust authorizes the holder to proceed with foreclosure to enforce the terms of the deed of trust. The dollar amount secured by the deed of trust or mortgage lien is often tied to the difference between the market price and the subsidized purchase price.

Another method of preserving affordability upon resale is through the formation of a community land trust.[14] In a community land trust, a nonprofit entity owns a parcel of land and housing on that land. The nonprofit then *leases* the land (typically through a very inexpensive ninety-nine-year ground lease) and *sells* the improvements (that is, the dwelling) to a qualifying household. The ground lease restricts the price at which the house may be sold to a subsequent purchaser.[15]

Whether to allow these control mechanisms to lapse in the event of a foreclosure of an inclusionary unit's primary mortgage lien is an additional policy decision. Some lenders will demand that transfer controls be allowed to lapse upon foreclosure, while other lenders will support the survival of the controls. Communities that wish to ensure that the transfer controls survive a foreclosure of the primary mortgage lien should design the process for recordation of the control mechanism in consultation with a real estate attorney. Generally, the transfer controls will survive foreclosure of a mortgage lien only if they have been recorded in the appropriate land records prior to the recordation of the mortgage lien and have not been subordinated to that lien.[16]

EXAMPLES

Kill Devil Hills secures affordability by recording a deed of trust in favor of the town.

> *Deed of trust.* The restrictive covenants and the applicant's or its successor's obligation to comply with the terms of this section shall be secured by a deed of trust in favor of the town, in a form satisfactory to the town. Such deed of trust shall be recorded prior to the issuance of an occupancy permit. The town shall subordinate the deed of trust to the lien of any lender financing the purchase of any of the housing units, upon proof of compliance with the terms of this section and upon certification from the OBCDC [Outer Banks Community Development Corporation, a non-profit community development organization in Dare County], or its successor, of compliance with the Housing Placement Eligibility System [a system, described in the deed of trust, for placing eligible persons in inclusionary units], as it may be amended from time to time. Violation of the terms of this section or the terms of the restrictive covenants required above, shall be an event of default under the terms of such deed of trust and shall authorize the town, in addition to any other remedy available, to foreclose upon the property as provided in the deed of trust.
>
> TOWN OF KILL DEVIL HILLS, N.C., CODE OF ORDINANCES § 153.207(H) (2008)

Santa Fe requires that a deed restriction be used to secure future affordability of the for-sale homes produced by its Santa Fe Homes Program (SFHP).

> A. An SFHP developer selling a SFHP home or manufactured home lot shall cause to be recorded, in the county clerk's office, simultaneous with the recording of the deed of sale, a form of deed restriction, restrictive covenant or other legal instrument . . .
>
> Santa Fe, N.M., City Code § 26-1.18 (2009)

However, in the event that the deed restriction is overlooked, Santa Fe also backstops the restriction by requiring that an affordability lien be placed on the property. The lien secures a dollar amount equal to the difference between the market value of the unit and the affordable price at which the unit was sold.

> A. . . . In order to maintain affordability, the SFHP developer shall impose resale controls consisting of mortgage liens, which include shared appreciation described below, and right of first refusal requirements as set forth in the administrative procedures. The effect of the recordation of said document(s) shall be to create, in accordance with state law, an obligation that runs with the property. The city shall approve the form of such documents prior to recordation. Initial affordability shall be achieved by including in the SFHP agreement terms of an escrow instruction requiring certification of SFHP compliance by the escrow agent.
>
> B. The amount of the above-described lien will be the difference between the SFHP price and the initial market value of the SFHP home or SFHP manufactured home lot. In order to provide additional equity to the SFHP buyer at the time of purchase, the initial market value shall be determined as ninety-five percent (95%) of the appraised value of the SFHP home or SFHP manufactured home lot.
>
> . . .
>
> D. Upon resale of an SFHP home or manufactured home lot, the affordability lien may be assumed by another SFHP buyer as approved by the city or its agent, or the seller must repay the SFHP lien to the city or its agent.
>
> Santa Fe, N.M., City Code § 26-1.18 (2009)

Right of First Refusal

A number of inclusionary zoning programs give the local government or other management authority a right of first refusal to purchase an affordable unit when it is offered for resale. This permits the local government either to purchase the unit itself or to find an eligible buyer (or other entity that agrees to preserve the unit's affordability) and assign its purchase right to that buyer. The unit is thus kept off the open market, and its affordability protections remain intact.

Questions to be addressed in developing a right of first refusal include the following:

- Who is entitled to the right of first refusal?
- What notice should be required?
- What is an appropriate length for the response period?
- What price should be used (market price or "affordable" price)?
- How should homeowner divorces be handled?

EXAMPLES

Burlington requires that the city be notified and given the option to purchase an inclusionary unit before it is offered for sale.

> Purchase Option. Provisions for continued affordability of inclusionary units shall provide that the Housing Trust Fund Administrative Committee or its designee shall have an exclusive option to purchase any inclusionary unit when it is offered for resale for a period of one hundred twenty (120) days from the date on which the HTF [Housing Trust Fund] Administrative Committee is notified of the availability of the unit;
>
> CITY OF BURLINGTON, VT., COMPREHENSIVE DEVELOPMENT ORDINANCE § 9.1.17(e) (2009)

Montgomery County shares in the profit upon resale of a unit, so it requires that the county be notified and given a sixty-day window in which to exercise its right of first refusal whenever an inclusionary unit (MPDU) is to be resold.

Resale Procedures.

(a) The Department, its designee, or the Commission has the right to purchase any resale MPDU. The owner must offer the MPDU for resale only to the Department, or to eligible certificate holders, during the first 60 days following the owner's notification to the Department. The County may assign its right to purchase the unit to a designated housing provider or to an eligible certificate holder.

. . .

(c) The Department must notify the owner within the 60 day period whether or not the Department intends to purchase the unit, and of any other conditions of the sale. If the MPDU is not purchased by the Department, its designee, or the Commission, the Department must notify the owner of the method that must be used to sell the unit.

(d) If the resale MPDU is purchased by the Department or its designee, or the Commission, these agencies may retain the MPDU or make it available to eligible certificate holders through a lottery or other means as may be approved by the Department.

. . .

(i) The MPDU may be offered to the general public at the approved maximum resale price only after the 60 day marketing period to the Department, its designee, the Commission, and all eligible certificate holders has expired. The owner must not offer MPDUs to the general public unless the priority marketing period has ended, the lottery list of all eligible certificate holders has been exhausted, and a written notice has been obtained from the Department authorizing sale to the general public. The priority marketing period is automatically extended unless the Department determines that no additional eligible persons are available to purchase the MPDUs.

MONTGOMERY COUNTY, MD., CODE REGS. (COMCOR) § 25A.00.02.08.3 (2003)

The county also retains a right of first refusal over the first resale after the control period expires.

Resale of MPDUs After the Control Period

9.1 Seller's Notification of the Department. For the first sale of an MPDU after the expiration of the applicable control period, the owner must provide the following information to the Department 30 days prior to settlement:

(a) A copy of the signed sales contract which clearly states the agreed upon sales price;

(b) A copy of the real estate broker's listing agreement;

(c) An itemized list of improvements including actual or estimated value of the improvements with documentation of the value in a form acceptable to the Department; and

(d) The name and contact information for the settlement agent, once it has been determined.

9.2 Commission's Right to Purchase MPDUs. The Department must immediately notify the Commission of the offer, and the Commission must have the right to match the purchase offer. The Commission must notify the Department and the owner within 14 days of the Department's receipt of notification of the offer, whether or not it intends to purchase the unit. If the Commission decides to exercise its right to purchase the MPDU, it must tender a purchase contract to the owner within 21 days from the date it notifies the Department and owner of its decision. The offer must contain substantially the same terms and conditions, and a deposit must be made, payable to an escrow agent. If within 14 days of the Department's receipt of the offering notice, the owner does not receive written notice from the Commission that it intends to purchase the unit, or if after receiving such notice, the owner does not receive from the Commission a purchase contract at the price and terms substantially comparable to the offer within 21 days, the owner shall be free to execute the prior contract at the price and terms originally offer[ed].

MONTGOMERY COUNTY, MD., CODE REGS. (COMCOR) § 25A.00.02.09 (2003)

However, Montgomery County exempts buyouts that are the result of a divorce settlement from the County's right of first refusal.

9.4 Divorce. If one owner buys out the other owner's interest in the unit as part of a divorce settlement, without selling the unit on the open market, then this does not constitute the first sale of the unit, and does not relieve the remaining owner of the shared profit obligation.

MONTGOMERY COUNTY, MD., CODE REGS. (COMCOR) § 25A.00.02.09 (2003)

Equity Sharing

To balance the need to preserve the affordability of inclusionary units and the desire to provide owners with some of the benefits of homeownership, some communities employ an equity sharing arrangement upon resale of owner-occupied affordable housing units. These arrangements vary greatly from program to program,[17] but generally, they allow the homeowner to keep a percentage of the appreciation in the property upon resale, as well as the cost of any improvements made by the resident.[18] Simple methods of equity sharing are illustrated in the examples at the end of this subsection, although an exhaustive treatment of equity sharing is beyond the scope of this publication.

Many equity sharing arrangements are secured by one of the two following methods:

- A lien on the property (see "Deed Restrictions, Deeds of Trust, and Ground Leases," above)
- A ground lease, in which the owner owns only the building and leases the land from the municipality or a nonprofit organization such as a community land trust[19]

EXAMPLES

Napa's equity sharing formula involves adjusting the purchase price to reflect the change in median income in the community. It also allows the purchase price to include the cost of any improvements made by the owner and a reasonable broker's fee.

(a) The maximum sales price permitted on resale of an affordable unit intended for owner-occupancy shall not exceed the seller's purchase price, adjusted for the percentage increase in median income since the seller's purchase, plus the value of substantial structural or permanent fixed improvements to the property, plus the cost of reasonable seller's broker fee as determined by the housing director.

(b) the resale restrictions shall provide that in the event of the sale of an affordable unit intended for owner-occupancy, the city shall have the right to purchase or assign its right to purchase such affordable unit at the maximum price which could be charged to an eligible household. [note that a purchase by the city would still occur at the maximum price, which would allow the prior owner to retain the same equity that he or she would have retained had the property been sold to another eligible household]

CITY OF NAPA, CAL., MUN. CODE § 15.94.050(J)(2) (2005)

The Santa Fe Homes Program (SFHP) employs an equity sharing formula based on the ratio of the subsidy to the initial market value of the home.

> An SFHP lien [required as part of the program and equal to the difference between 95% of the appraised value and the SFHP sales price] will provide for shared appreciation by requiring the buyer to repay the original amount of the lien plus a share of appreciation, if any, upon resale of the home or manufactured home lot or violation of the occupancy requirements as described herein and by the administrative procedures. The city's share of appreciation, if any, will be in proportion to the ratio of the SFHP lien to the initial market value at the time of the SFHP buyer's initial purchase. The administrative procedures shall provide for a deduction from gross appreciation to account for capital improvements and repairs made during time of ownership and for a proportion of closing costs incurred upon resale. For purpose of example, following are steps used to determine the city's share of appreciation:
>
> (1) Determine SFHP affordable home price (example: 3 bedroom home in income range 3 [between 65% and 80% of area median income): $142,000
>
> (2) Determine appraised value of SFHP home: $220,000
>
> (3) Determine initial market value of SFHP home: $220,000 X 95% = $209,000
>
> (4) Determine amount of lien: $209,000 - $142,000 = $67,000
>
> (5) Determine city's share of appreciation (proportion of lien to initial market value):
> $67,000/$209,000 = 32%
>
> SANTA FE, N.M., CITY CODE § 26-1.18(C) (2009)

San Diego applies a sliding scale percentage of equity sharing based on how long the resident has owned the unit.

> (3) The equity in the affordable unit shall be shared as follows:
> (A) Equity for purposes of this Division is measured by the difference in the original unrestricted fair market value of the affordable unit at the time of the acquisition of the affordable unit and the unrestricted fair market value of the affordable unit on the date of the first resale, and each and every transfer, lease or refinancing as determined by an appraisal approved by the City.

(B) Upon the first resale of the affordable unit during the first 15 years from the date of issuance of the certificate of occupancy, the City and owner of the affordable unit shall share the equity in accordance with the provisions of Table 142-13B.

(C) Upon each transfer, lease and or refinancing during the first 15 years from the date of issuance of the certificate of occupancy, the City and the Owner shall share the equity in the affordable unit based upon an appraisal of the affordable unit in accordance with the provisions of Table 142-13B.

(D) Upon any sale or any transfer, whenever it occurs the City shall also receive that sum which is calculated as the difference between the original fair market value of the affordable unit and the restricted value of the affordable unit at the time of the original sale, as determined by an appraisal as approved by the City.

. . .

TABLE 142-13B

Length of Ownership at the Time of Resale, Refinance, or Transfer	Share of Equity to Household
Months 0–12	15%
Year 2	21
Year 3	27
Year 4	33
Year 5	39
Year 6	45
Year 7	51
Year 8	57
Year 9	63
Year 10	69
Year 11	75
Year 12	81
Year 13	87
Year 14	93
Year 15 or after	100%

CITY OF SAN DIEGO, CAL., MUN. CODE § 142.1309(e) (2008)

Burlington, on the other hand, provides that a seller may retain a set percentage of the unit's increase in value.

> Resale Restrictions. Provisions to ensure continued affordability of inclusionary units offered for sale shall include a formula for limiting equity appreciation to an amount not to exceed twenty-five percent (25%) of the increase in the inclusionary unit's value, as determined by the difference between fair market appraisal at the time of purchase of the property and a fair market appraisal at the time of resale, with such adjustments for improvements made by the seller and necessary costs of sale as may be approved by the Manager, with a recommendation from the Administrative Committee of the HTF [Housing Trust Fund];
>
> CITY OF BURLINGTON, VT., COMPREHENSIVE DEVELOPMENT ORDINANCE § 9.1.17(c) (2009)

Leasing and Subleasing

Even if an affordable housing unit is sold or rented to a qualifying household, that owner or renter may in some cases attempt to lease (or sublease) the unit out to a nonqualified household. A number of inclusionary zoning ordinances therefore require that ownership covenants or rental agreements include clauses that prohibit rental (of for-sale affordable units) or subletting (of for-rent affordable units).[20]

Enforcement of these controls may take a variety of forms, including the following:

- Brief home visits, at which a representative of the management agency comes to the front door and confirms that the proper household is residing in the unit
- A periodic letter or affidavit that must be signed and returned
- Provision of a means for neighbors to report violations of the occupancy restrictions

EXAMPLES

San Diego requires all for-sale inclusionary units to be occupied by their owners. If this owner-occupancy provision is violated, the owner-lessor is subject to a recapture of equity.

> Affordable Units must be owner occupied unless the San Diego Housing Commission has determined a hardship on a case-by-case

basis. Except where authorized by the San Diego Housing Commission for a specific unit, renting a restricted unit would trigger a recapture in equity pursuant to San Diego Municipal Code Section 142.1309(e) [*i.e., the city would be entitled to its share of the equity in the project, as measured by a city-designed formula*].

CITY OF SAN DIEGO, CAL., INCLUSIONARY AFFORDABLE HOUS. IMPLEMENTATION & MONITORING PROCEDURES MANUAL 2 (revised Mar. 2008)

Santa Fe, likewise, prohibits leasing of any of the properties constructed pursuant to its Santa Fe Homes Program (SFHP), except in cases of exceptional hardship.

An SFHP home buyer or SFHP manufactured home lot buyer shall not rent the SFHP unit or manufactured home lot to a second party, except as approved in writing by the office of affordable housing for instances in which the owner is under duress by reason of unemployment, family medical emergencies, or inability to sell the home for an amount equal to or greater than the original sale price, or other unique circumstances of family hardship.

SANTA FE, N.M., CITY CODE § 26-1.18(F) (2009)

Fairfax County requires that renters and owners of affordable housing units provided by its program annually execute an affidavit that confirms their occupancy of the unit.

Purchasers or renters of affordable dwelling units shall occupy the units as their domicile and shall provide an executed affidavit on an annual basis certifying their continuing occupancy of the units. Owners of for sale affordable dwelling units shall forward such affidavit to the Fairfax County Redevelopment and Housing Authority on or before June 1 of each year that they own the unit. Renters shall provide such affidavit to their landlords/owners by the date that may be specified in their lease or that may otherwise be specified by the landlord/owner.

COUNTY OF FAIRFAX, VA., ZONING ORDINANCE § 2-813(5) (2009)

Marketing of Inclusionary Units

To ensure that the intended households have adequate opportunity to purchase or rent an inclusionary unit, several inclusionary zoning programs impose marketing requirements upon developers, sometimes in conjunction with rights of first refusal. The simplest marketing requirement designates a marketing period during which a developer must market an inclusionary unit only to eligible households.

EXAMPLES

Montgomery County designates a priority marketing period during which the developer (or applicant) must market a moderately priced dwelling unit (MPDU) only to those individuals holding a certificate of eligibility for such units.

> 1.26. "Priority marketing period" means a period of no more than 90 days from the date the Department gives the Applicant an approved list of eligible certificate holders to whom the units may be marketed, during which time the MPDU must be available exclusively to persons holding a Certificate of Eligibility under the program.
>
> MONTGOMERY COUNTY, MD., CODE REGS. (COMCOR) § 25A.00.02.01 (2003)

If units are not sold to eligible persons by the end of the marketing period, the county's Department of Housing and Community Development may approve sale to the general public. Separate marketing requirements are provided for rental units.

> (e) Eligible certificate holders selected by a lottery must have the exclusive right to enter into a contract for the purchase of an MPDU. The priority marketing period begins the day the Offering Agreement is approved by the Department, or the date of the Department's approval of other marketing methods, and must end 90 days after the date of commencement.
>
> (f) The applicant must not offer MPDUs to the general public unless the priority marketing period has ended, the lottery list of all eligible certificate holders has been exhausted, and a written notice has been obtained from the Department authorizing the sale to the general public. The priority marketing period is automatically extended unless the Department determines that no additional eligible persons are

> available to purchase the MPDUs. MPDUs that become available for
> sale after the priority marketing period because of the disapproval of
> permanent loan financing must be offered to eligible certificate hold-
> ers on the lottery list. MPDUs that are offered to the general public
> remain subject to all the regulations and laws governing the Program,
> except the income limitations.
>
> Montgomery County, Md., Code Regs. (COMCOR) § 25A.00.02.06.6.2 (2003)

Notes

1. See "Takings" in the Legal Appendix.

2. *See* Business and Professional People for the Public Interest, Opening the Door to Inclusionary Zoning 41–42 (2003) (hereinafter BPI). Montgomery County, MD, Fairfax County, VA, and Burlington, VT, have a history of keeping
local housing nonprofits closely involved in the management and operation of inclusionary
zoning units.

3. An agreement between the local government and a nonprofit might have the added
benefit of avoiding a violation of North Carolina's rent control ban. See "North Carolina
Limitation on Rent Control" in the Legal Appendix.

4. North Carolina local governments seeking to impose the penalties described in this
example should consult a local government or land use attorney regarding authority to do
so. See Chapter 6, note 1.

5. *See* Saenz v. Roe, 526 U.S. 489 (1999) ("The word 'travel' is not found in the text of
the Constitution. Yet the "constitutional right to travel from one State to another" is firmly
embedded in our jurisprudence. *United States v. Guest*, 383 U.S. 745, 757 (1966)."). Courts
have found that some durational residency requirements interfere with that right, although
there are a number of inclusionary zoning ordinances that contain durational requirements. Those that do contain durational requirements must show (often through preamble
language) that the requirement is narrowly tailored to meet a compelling government
purpose. To the extent that a local government imposes regulatory requirements on private
housing owners as a means of effecting a preference for local residents, it will more likely
be viewed as running afoul of the Commerce Clause. However, when a local government
operates as a market participant—for example, by owning and operating its own housing units—a local preference will rest on firmer ground. *See, e.g.*, White v. Massachusetts
Council of Construction Employers, Inc., 460 U.S. 204 (1983).

6. U.S. Const. art. IV, § 2, cl. 1 ("The Citizens of each State shall be entitled to all
Privileges and Immunities of Citizens in the several States."). Courts have found that
some durational residency requirements interfere with the Privileges and Immunities

Clause, particularly restrictions that deal with creating jobs specifically for local residents. *See* David M. Lawrence, Economic Development Law for North Carolina Local Governments 58–59 (UNC Institute of Government 2000) (citing a number of U.S. Court of Appeals cases brought by construction unions against residency-restricted jobs). A principal question in applying this case law is whether the opportunity to purchase or rent an inclusionary home is "sufficiently basic to the livelihood of the Nation" to fall within the clause's purview. *See* Baldwin v. Montana Fish and Game Comm'n, 436 U.S. 371, 388 (1978). Although normally applied to actions by state governments, the Privileges and Immunities Clause might also apply to local governments. *See* Building Trades v. Mayor and Council of Camden, 465 U.S. 208, 216–17 (1984) ("A person who is not residing in a given State is ipso facto not residing in a city within that State. Thus, whether the exercise of a privilege is conditioned on state residency or on municipal residency, he will just as surely be excluded.").

7. See "Equal Protection" in the Legal Appendix.

8. *See, e.g.,* City & County of Denver, Colo., Rev. Mun. Code § 27-103(h) (2009), *available at* www.municode.com/Resources/gateway.asp?pid=10257&sid=6.

9. See, for example, City of Burlington, Vt., Comprehensive Development Ordinance § 9.1.17(a) (2009), which is included in the examples below.

10. See, for example, Town of Manteo, N.C., Zoning Code § 11-12 (2009), which is included in the examples below.

11. *See* California Affordable Housing Law Project & Western Center on Law and Poverty, Inclusionary Zoning: Policy Considerations and Best Practices 37 (2002).

12. *See* Enterprise Community Partners, Inclusionary Zoning: Program Design Considerations 2 (2004); BPI, note 2 above, at 10.

13. *See, e.g.*, City of Burlington, Vt., Comprehensive Development Ordinance § 9.1.17 (2009), which is included in the examples below.

14. *See generally* Julie F. Curtin and Lance Bocarsly, *CLTs: A Growing Trend in Affordable Home Ownership*, 17 J. Affordable Housing & Comm. Dev. L. 367 (2008).

15. The community land trust model is often used to allow for some equity sharing with owners of inclusionary units upon resale. That aspect is discussed in "Equity Sharing," below.

16. In North Carolina, a foreclosure sale by a trustee in a junior deed of trust is made subject to prior liens on the property. Staunton Military Academy, Inc. v. Dockery, 244 N.C. 427, 430, 94 S.E.2d 354, 356–57 (1956). *See also* St. Louis Union Trust Co. v. Foster, 211 N.C. 331, 190 S.E. 522 (1937) ("The title of the purchaser at a sale under a decree of foreclosure relates back to the date of the delivery of the mortgage. . . . All incumbrances and liens, and all conditions, reservations and restrictions which the mortgagor may have imposed upon the property subsequently to the execution of the mortgage, will be extinguished." (citing Wiltsie on Mortgage Foreclosure, Vol. 2 (4th ed.) 1030–31)).

17. For an example of a more complex equity-sharing arrangement established as part of an inclusionary zoning ordinance, see Montgomery County, Md., Code Regs.

(COMCOR) § 25A.00.02.08.2 (2003), *available at* www.amlegal.com/library/md/montgomeryco.shtml.

18. For more on equity sharing and how it works, see CENTER FOR HOUSING POLICY, USE SHARED EQUITY MECHANISMS TO PRESERVE HOMEOWNERSHIP SUBSIDIES, *available at* www.housingpolicy.org/toolbox/strategy/policies/shared_equity.html; JESSE MINTZ-ROTH, LONG-TERM AFFORDABLE HOUSING STRATEGIES IN HOT HOUSING MARKETS (Harvard Joint Center for Housing Studies, 2008), *available at* www.jchs.harvard.edu/publications/homeownership/w08-3_mintz-roth.pdf. *See also* RICK JACOBUS, CENTER FOR HOUSING POLICY, SHARED EQUITY, TRANSFORMATIVE WEALTH (2007), *available at* www.rjacobus.com/resources/archives/papers/000425.html. A more exhaustive discussion of equity sharing is contained in JOHN EMMEUS DAVIS, NATIONAL HOUSING INSTITUTE, SHARED EQUITY HOMEOWNERSHIP: THE CHANGING LANDSCAPE OF RESALE-RESTRICTED, OWNER-OCCUPIED HOUSING (2006), *available at* www.nhi.org/pdf/SharedEquityHome.pdf.

19. This describes the community land trust model explained in "Deed Restrictions, Deeds of Trust, and Ground Leases," above.

20. Programs requiring owners to occupy units should be drafted with caution in North Carolina. It is likely permissible through private contractual restrictions (e.g., through recordation of a deed of trust or deed restriction) to require a qualified purchaser to occupy a purchased inclusionary unit. Nonetheless, policy makers should remain mindful of North Carolina Court of Appeal decisions that have struck down attempts by local governments to use general zoning ordinances to require owners to occupy their homes. See "Consistent Tenancy or Manner of Ownership" in Chapter 6.

Legal Appendix

This appendix reviews the legal status of inclusionary zoning programs generally, as well as the most significant legal issues that such ordinances might confront in North Carolina. Part 1 examines under what circumstances, if any, implementation of an inclusionary zoning ordinance might interfere with rights protected by the United States and North Carolina Constitutions. Part 2 examines specific issues under North Carolina law: the extent to which local governments have the authority to engage in inclusionary zoning in North Carolina, and what implications North Carolina's ban on rent control ordinances might have for inclusionary zoning.

Part 1: Constitutional Considerations

There are three principal constitutional issues raised by the adoption of an inclusionary zoning program. This part describes the implications of (1) the prohibition against the taking of private property without just compensation, (2) the requirements of due process, and (3) equal protection under the law. These issues may arise under either the United States Constitution or the North Carolina Constitution; subtle differences in the state and federal legal tests will be discussed in the sections relating to each issue.

Takings

The Fifth Amendment to the United States Constitution prevents governments from taking private property for public use without just compensation.[1] In the context of inclusionary zoning, the concern is that a particular affordable housing set-aside may unreasonably deprive the developer of some of the economic value of the development or appropriate some of the units. Ultimately, the claim amounts to little, as a takings challenge to an inclusionary zoning program is unlikely to succeed in court.[2]

Takings challenges can take either of two approaches: a program may be challenged as constituting a taking on its face—that is, as invalid in any and every application—or it may be challenged as constituting a taking as applied to a particular situation. Courts are unlikely to find an inclusionary zoning program to be invalid on its face, as this requires that the ordinance constitute a taking in every instance for every project. In fact, at least one court has held that where the local government preserves the right to waive an inclusionary zoning program's requirements, the program *cannot*, on its face, result in a taking.[3] Partly for this reason, inclusionary zoning programs often contain clauses allowing for waivers or other hardship measures.[4]

Even when a program is not an unconstitutional taking on its face, it may be challenged as being a taking in the way it is applied to a particular person

---

1. U.S. Const. amend. V (". . . nor shall private property be taken for public use, without just compensation.").

2. *See* Laura M. Padilla, *Reflections on Inclusionary Housing and a Renewed Look at its Viability*, 23 Hofstra L. Rev. 539, 597–603 (1995).

3. *See* Home Builders Ass'n of Northern California v. City of Napa, 90 Cal. App. 4th 188, 194 (Cal. Ct. App. 2001).

4. See Chapter 5.

or situation. In response to such an as-applied challenge, the court will examine the ordinance's impact in that particular situation.

The U.S. Supreme Court has established three bases for takings challenges: physical takings, regulatory takings, and land-use exactions.[5] Each will be discussed in turn.

Physical Takings

In some instances, a government action is always considered a taking of property. These types of takings are called *per se* takings, since they always require the government to provide compensation. The clearest case of a *per se* taking is the "permanent physical occupation"[6] of all or part of a parcel of property. For instance, in *Loretto v. Teleprompter Manhattan CATV Corp.*, the U.S. Supreme Court ruled that a law requiring the installation of a cable converter and crossover cables, taking up "about one-eighth of a cubic foot of space," was a taking because the cable equipment constituted a permanent physical invasion, regardless of its small size (and the commensurately small compensation the landowner would receive).[7]

In order for an inclusionary zoning ordinance to constitute a physical invasion of property, the local government would likely have to take title to the affordable units produced under the program. Most of the inclusionary zoning ordinances surveyed for this publication leave inclusionary units in private hands and regulate how those units may be used; they typically do not require that the owner surrender title to the affordable units.

Regulatory Takings

Less clear than the physical taking is the so-called regulatory taking,[8] wherein the court examines all of an owner's rights in the land to determine whether the government has eliminated enough of the owner's rights for the courts to

---

5. Lingle v. Chevron U.S.A., Inc., 544 U.S. 528, 548 (2005) ("[A] plaintiff seeking to challenge a government regulation as an uncompensated taking of private property may proceed under one of the other theories discussed above—by alleging a 'physical' taking, a *Lucas*-type 'total regulatory taking,' a *Penn Central* taking, or a land-use exaction violating the standards set forth in *Nollan* and *Dolan*.").

6. Loretto v. Teleprompter Manhattan CATV Corp., 458 U.S. 419, 420 (1982).

7. *Id*. at 438 n.16.

8. "The general rule, at least, is that, while property may be regulated to a certain extent, if regulation goes too far, it will be recognized as a taking." Pennsylvania Coal Co. v. Mahon, 260 U.S. 393, 415 (1922).

conclude that the government action was "tantamount to a condemnation or appropriation" of the land.[9]

The only *per se* regulatory taking (that is, the only case in which a restriction of use that does not involve a physical invasion is *always* considered a taking) occurs when the regulation deprives an owner of all economically viable use of his or her property, when that property is viewed as a whole.[10] It is virtually impossible for an inclusionary zoning ordinance to run afoul of this test, as no inclusionary zoning program would be designed to deprive an owner of all economically viable use of his or her land.[11] After all, inclusionary zoning is dependent upon successful market-rate developments in order to be put into effect.

Those cases that do not involve a physical invasion or a deprivation of all economic use will be analyzed under the three-factor balancing test for regulatory takings laid out in the U.S. Supreme Court's landmark decision in *Penn Central Transportation Co. v. New York City.*[12] *Penn Central* requires that a court consider (1) the economic impact of the government regulation on the landowner, (2) the extent to which the regulation interferes with the landowner's reasonable investment-backed expectations, and (3) whether the character of the government action resembles a physical appropriation.[13]

---

9. Tahoe-Sierra Pres. Council v. Tahoe Reg'l Planning Agency, 535 U.S. 302, 322 n.17 (2002).

10. Lucas v. S.C. Coastal Council, 505 U.S. 1003, 1015 (1992) ("The second situation in which we have found categorical treatment appropriate is where regulation denies all economically beneficial or productive use of land."); Concrete Pipe & Prods. v. Constr. Laborers Pension Trust, 508 U.S. 602 (1993).

11. It takes an extremely unlikely scenario to provide an example of how an inclusionary zoning program might conceivably deprive an owner of all economically feasible use of his or her property. If a parcel of land had no feasible use but residential development, and if zoning regulations required the owner to build an overwhelming number of affordable housing units for which no buyers or tenants existed—and therefore the units would never be sold or rented—then perhaps in that case, the owner could show that such a development would constitute a total deprivation.

12. 438 U.S. 104 (1978).

13. Penn Central Transp. Co. v. New York City, 438 U.S. 104, 124 (1978); *see also* Serena M. Williams, *The Need for Affordable Housing: The Constitutional Viability of Inclusionary Zoning,* 26 J. MARSHALL L. REV. 75, 89 (1992). Each of the factors must be considered, and none can be dispositive in and of itself. *See Penn Central,* 438 U.S. at 131 ("[T]he decisions sustaining other land use regulations, which . . . are reasonably related

The first factor focuses on the impact of the regulation on the owner's ability to earn economic rewards from the property. However, short of the kind of full deprivation found in the *Lucas* case discussed above, a diminution in property value or economic return is highly unlikely to result in a finding that the regulation rises to the level of a taking.[14]

The investment-backed expectations protected by the second factor are those that have been *reasonably* relied on in making investment decisions.[15] What expectations are reasonable may depend upon such considerations as the current use of the property[16] and what was allowed under the regulations in effect when the property was purchased.[17] However, this factor does not require that an owner be able to earn the maximum return possible from the land or a return equal to what he or she would have obtained without the challenged program in place.[18]

There is no bright-line rule to establish at what point a diminution in value is sufficient to violate a developer's expectations. As a precautionary measure, local governments may seek to compensate for some diminution in value resulting from an inclusionary zoning ordinance by providing

---

to the promotion of the general welfare, uniformly reject the proposition that diminution in property value, standing alone, can establish a 'taking.'"), and *Palazzolo v. Rhode Island*, 533 U.S. 606, 634 ("Investment-backed expectations, though important, are not talismanic under *Penn Central*. Evaluation of the degree of interference with investment-backed expectations instead is one factor that points toward the answer to the question whether the application of a particular regulation to particular property 'goes too far.'") (O'Connor, J., concurring).

14. *Penn Central*, 438 U.S. at 131, notes some of the substantial diminutions in property value in cases in which a taking was not found, including *Euclid v. Ambler Realty Co.*, 272 U.S. 365 (1926) (75 percent diminution in value caused by zoning law); and *Hadacheck v. Sebastian*, 239 U.S. 394 (1915) (87.5 percent diminution in value). *See also* Williams, note 13 above, at 89.

15. The expectation "must be more than a 'unilateral expectation or an abstract need.'" Ruckelshaus v. Monsanto, 467 U.S. 986, 1005 (1984).

16. *See Penn Central* at 136 (explaining that challenged law allowed claimants to "continue to use the property precisely as it has been used for the past 65 years: . . . So the law does not interfere with what must be regarded as Penn Central's primary expectation concerning the use of the parcel.").

17. *See* Palazzolo v. Rhode Island, 533 U.S. 606, 633–35 (2001) ("[T]he regulatory regime in place at the time the claimant acquires the property at issue helps to shape the reasonableness of those expectations.") (O'Connor, J., concurring).

18. *Penn Central*, 438 U.S. at 130–31; *see also* Williams, note 13 above, at 89.

density bonuses, streamlined permitting, or lower site-improvement fees. Additionally, a study demonstrating that an inclusionary zoning ordinance will continue to allow developers an economically viable use of property should prove helpful in meeting this standard.[19]

The third factor of the *Penn Central* test considers the "character of the government action"; namely, whether it seems more like a "physical invasion" rather than simply being "some public program adjusting the benefits and burdens of economic life to promote the common good."[20] However, this prong of the analysis has been overshadowed by the subsequent decisions in *Loretto* and *Lucas*, such that it is now largely a question of whether the government action is reasonably justified.[21]

Exactions

When an owner is required to make a dedication of property for the benefit of the public—for example, a dedication of recreational space—as a condition of land use approval for a particular development, the dedication is generally referred to as an exaction. As a matter of U.S. constitutional law, exactions must be related—in the Court's words, they must possess an "essential nexus"[22]—to the end being sought. Additionally, when applied to a particular development, exactions must exhibit a "rough proportionality"[23] to the impacts of the expected use.

----

19. For a defense of this point, see Barbara Ehrlich Kautz, *In Defense of Inclusionary Zoning: Successfully Creating Affordable Housing*, 36 U.S.F. L. REV. 971, 1009–10 (2002) ("So long as the adoption of an inclusionary ordinance is accompanied by an economic study demonstrating that the requirements are reasonable and allow an economically viable use, it is highly unlikely that a *Penn Central* challenge will be able to establish a substantial economic impact or interference with reasonable investment-backed expectations").

20. *Penn Central*, 438 U.S. at 124 ("A 'taking' may more readily be found when the interference with property can be characterized as a physical invasion by government, *see, e.g., United States v. Causby*, 328 U. S. 256 (1946), than when interference arises from some public program adjusting the benefits and burdens of economic life to promote the common good.").

21. Andre Peterson, *The Takings Clause: In Search of Underlying Principles*, 77 CAL. L. REV. 1301, 1319 (1989) ("[I]n [*Keystone Bituminous Coal Ass'n v. DeBenedictis*, 480 U.S. 470 (1987)] . . . the Court moved from asking whether the government had imposed a serious loss on the claimant to asking whether the government's actions were justified.").

22. Nollan v. Cal. Coastal Comm'n, 483 U.S. 825, 837 (1987).

23. Dolan v. City of Tigard, 512 U.S. 374 (1994) (requiring that an exaction be "roughly proportional" to the impact of the proposed development). The court in *Dolan* emphasized that "[N]o precise mathematical calculation is required," but the local govern-

When a general dedication requirement applies to all developments—as opposed to being negotiated on a case-by-case basis—the dedication remains subject to takings analysis but not to the exactions standards described above.[24] In a significant case testing inclusionary zoning, a California appeals court panel evaluated a generally applicable mandatory inclusionary zoning program and refused to apply the "essential nexus" and "rough proportionality" standards on the basis that the program was generally applicable.[25] In the event an inclusionary zoning–related dedication is evaluated as an exaction, the nexus and proportionality tests could be satisfied through a study demonstrating a connection between the construction of market-rate housing and the need for affordable housing. A common argument, for example, is that a commercial development or market-rate residential development adds new residents to a community. These new residents create demand for new commercial establishments, and those commercial establishments employ low- and moderate-income workers.[26] The inclusionary units, therefore, meet the additional housing demand created by the development. Such studies can provide the strongest legal defense to an exactions-related takings claim.[27]

---

ment "must make some sort of individualized determination that the required dedication is related both in nature and extent to the impact of the proposed development." *Id.* at 391.

24. *See* City of Monterey v. Del Monte Dunes at Monterey, Ltd., 526 U.S. 687, 702 (1999) ("[W]e have not extended the rough-proportionality test of *Dolan* beyond the special context of exactions—land-use decisions conditioning approval of development on the dedication of property to public use.").

25. Home Builders Ass'n v. City of Napa, 90 Cal. App. 4th 188 (2001), *cert. denied,* 533 U.S. 954 (2002). The court in *City of Napa* held that the heightened *Nollan/Dolan* standard does not apply where the challenged legislation is "generally applicable to all development in [the] city." *Id.* at 197. Citing prior decisions by the California Supreme Court, the *City of Napa* court pointed out that the *Nollan/Dolan* standard "is intended to address . . . land use 'bargains' between property owners and regulatory bodies—those in which the local government conditions permit approval for a given use on the owner's surrender of benefits which purportedly offset the impact of the proposed development," *id.* at 196 (quoting Ehrlich v. City of Culver City, 911 P.2d 429 (Cal. 1996)), and that generally applicable laws did not carry the risk of "extortionate" use of the police power. *See also* Barbara Ehrlich Kautz, *In Defense of Inclusionary Zoning: Successfully Creating Affordable Housing,* 36 U.S.F.L. Rev. 971, 1008 (2002) ("[O]nly if a local inclusionary ordinance requires developers to negotiate individually, with meaningful discretion applied by the government, would *Nollan/Dolan* apply to a particular project.").

26. *See* Thomas Kleven, *Inclusionary Ordinances—Policy and Legal Issues in Requiring Private Developers to Build Low Cost Housing,* 21 UCLA L. Rev. 1432, 1436 (1974).

27. For more considerations when commissioning a nexus study, see "Conducting a Housing Needs Assessment" in Chapter 1.

Takings in North Carolina

Although the North Carolina Constitution does not contain an express prohibition against the taking of property without just compensation, the North Carolina Supreme Court has recognized that the "law of the land" clause[28] in the North Carolina Constitution infers a similar restriction.[29]

Takings cases are relatively rare in North Carolina, and thus the case law based on the state's constitution is not as thoroughly developed as it is at the federal level.[30] However, North Carolina courts have historically shown a high degree of deference to zoning decisions.[31] In order to survive a takings claim based on the North Carolina Constitution, an ordinance must not render property valueless.[32] In addition, when an act is a proper exercise of the

---

28. N.C. Const. art. I, § 19 ("No person shall be taken, imprisoned, or disseized of his freehold, liberties, or privileges, or outlawed, or exiled, or in any manner deprived of his life, liberty, or property, but by the law of the land. No person shall be denied the equal protection of the laws; nor shall any person be subjected to discrimination by the State because of race, color, religion, or national origin.").

29. Finch v. City of Durham, 325 N.C. 352, 362–63, 384 S.E.2d 8, 14 (1989) ("We note initially that although the North Carolina Constitution does not contain an express provision prohibiting the taking of private property for public use without payment of just compensation, this Court has inferred such a provision as a fundamental right integral to the 'law of the land' clause in article I, section 19 of our Constitution." (citation omitted)).

30. See David W. Owens, Land Use Law in North Carolina 213 (UNC School of Government 2006) ("The taking issue has not been frequently litigated in North Carolina state courts. Only a handful of cases have addressed the issue to any substantial degree.").

31. See In re Parker, 214 N.C. 51, 55, 197 S.E. 706 (1938) ("When the most that can be said against such ordinances is that whether it was an unreasonable, arbitrary or unequal exercise of power is fairly debatable, the courts will not interfere. In such circumstances the settled rule seems to be that the court will not substitute its judgment for that of the legislative body charged with the primary duty and responsibility of determining whether its action is in the interest of the public health, safety, morals, or general welfare."); Kinney v. Sutton, 230 N.C. 404, 411–12, 53 S.E.2d 306, 311 (1949) ("[I]f the police power is properly exercised in the zoning of a municipality, a resultant pecuniary loss to a property owner is a misfortune which he must suffer as a member of society."); see also Owens, note 30 above, at 214–15.

32. In other words, the property must retain "a practical use and a reasonable value," *Finch*, 325 N.C. at 364, 384 S.E.2d at 15. This standard would be a difficult one for claimants to meet. See Helms v. City of Charlotte, 255 N.C. 647, 651, 122 S.E.2d 817, 820 (1961) ("The mere fact that a zoning ordinance seriously depreciates the value of the

police power, it will not be found to effect a taking.[33] Generally, an act is a proper exercise of the police power if the ends sought are within the scope of the police power and the means used are reasonable.[34]

Exactions in North Carolina

North Carolina law treats exactions in much the same way that they are treated under federal law. Any conditions or site-specific standards imposed must be limited to those that address the impacts reasonably expected to be generated by the development.[35]

Due Process

The Fourteenth Amendment to the United States Constitution provides, in part, that "[n]o state shall make or enforce any law which shall . . . deprive any person of life, liberty, or property, without due process of law."[36] There are two kinds of due process claims: substantive due process, which focuses on the justification for governmental action, and procedural due process, which requires adequate procedures before an individual is deprived of a significant interest involving life, liberty, or property.

---

complainant's property is not enough, standing alone, to establish its invalidity."). *See also* OWENS, note 30 above, at 214 n.32 and accompanying text.

33. Responsible Citizens v. City of Asheville, 308 N.C. 255, 302 S.E.2d 204 (1983) (". . . this court noted again that '(t)he question of what constitutes a taking is often interwoven with the question of whether a particular act is an exercise of the police power or of the power of eminent domain.' The Court also noted that '(i)f the act is a proper exercise of the police power, the constitutional provision that private property shall not be taken for public use, unless compensation is made, is not applicable.'" (quoting Department of Transp. v. Harkey, 308 N.C. 148, 301 S.E.2d 64(1983))).

34. *See Responsible Citizens*, 308 N.C. at 261–62, 302 S.E.2d at 209 ("The court first determines whether the ends sought, i.e., the object of the legislation, is within the scope of the [police] power. The court then determines whether the means chosen to regulate are reasonable . . . .[I]n determining if the means chosen are reasonable the court must answer the following: '(1) Is the statute in its application reasonably necessary to promote the accomplishment of a public good and (2) is the interference with the owner's right to use his property as he deems appropriate reasonable in degree?'" (quoting A-S-P Associates v. City of Raleigh, 298 N.C. 207, 258 S.E.2d 444 (1979))). *See also* OWENS, note 30 above, at 214 n.33 and accompanying text.

35. *See* N.C. GEN. STAT. (hereinafter G.S.) §§ 153A-342(b) and 160A-382(b). *See also* OWENS, note 30 above, at 40–41.

36. U.S. CONST. amend. XIV.

Substantive Due Process

The doctrine of substantive due process is designed to protect individuals from being unduly deprived of life, liberty, or property.[37] Substantive due process claims may be reviewed under one of two standards: a strict scrutiny standard or a rational basis standard. Whether a governmental action is reviewed under strict scrutiny or rational basis will have a highly significant and often determinative effect on the outcome of the case.

Certain fundamental rights, like the protections contained in the U.S. Constitution's Bill of Rights (the first ten amendments) and the political process, are considered "implicit in the concept of ordered liberty"[38] and receive special protection. Restrictions of these rights are reviewed under the strict scrutiny standard, which examines whether the restriction was narrowly tailored to achieve a compelling governmental purpose.[39] This is a high bar, and most regulations subject to strict scrutiny will be found to violate due process.

Most land use regulations, however, do not involve fundamental rights[40] and are instead reviewed under a less stringent rational basis standard. Under the rational basis standard, a zoning ordinance "would survive a substantive due process challenge so long as it was not 'clearly arbitrary and unreasonable, having no substantial relation to the public health, safety, morals, or general welfare.'"[41] When applying the rational basis test, a court first determines

---

37. Note that, in order for a property right to be the basis of a substantive due process claim, the claimant must have a "legitimate claim of entitlement" to the property. Board of Regents of State Colleges v. Roth, 408 U.S. 564, 577 (1972). Such a claim cannot, by definition, exist when the regulatory body retains some discretion over whether or not to permit a given use. DANIEL R. MANDELKER, LAND USE LAW § 2.45 (4th ed. 1997) (citing Sylvia Dev. Co. v. Calvert County, 48 F.3d 810 (4th Cir. 1995); Gardner v. City of Baltimore, 969 F.2d 63 (4th Cir. 1992)).

38. Palko v. Connecticut, 302 U.S. 319, 325 (1937).

39. *See, e.g.*, City of Boerne v. Flores, 521 U.S. 507 (1997).

40. *See, e.g.*, *Palko*, 302 U.S. 319, 324–27 (1937) (describing what makes a right fundamental); Capitol Outdoor, Inc. v. Tolson, 159 N.C. App. 55, 582 S.E.2d 717 (2003) (holding right to construct outdoor advertising is not fundamental).

41. Lingle v. Chevron U.S.A., Inc., 544 U.S. 528, 541 (2005) (quoting Euclid v. Ambler Realty Co., 272 U.S. 365, 395 (1926)). *See also* Usery v. Turner Elkhorn Mining Co., 428 U.S. 1, 15 ("[T]he burden is on one complaining of a due process violation to establish that the legislature has acted in an arbitrary and irrational way."); Summers v. City of Charlotte, 149 N.C. App. 509, 518, 562 S.E. 2d 18, 25, *review denied*, 355 N.C. 758, 566 S.E.2d 482

whether the regulation furthers a legitimate governmental interest.[42] As long as a legitimate interest exists, a court then looks to see whether there is any rational relationship between the burden imposed by the ordinance and the benefits conferred to the public and the affected party.[43] This standard is not difficult to overcome, and in making these determinations, courts give substantial deference to legislative decisions.[44] It is therefore difficult for a plaintiff to prevail on a due process claim when the rational basis test is applied.[45]

Procedural Due Process

Any adjudicative process established by an ordinance must comply with due process. As a threshold matter, due process requires some form of hearing before an individual is deprived of a property interest,[46] although the process required depends on the individual circumstances of each case.[47] The processes

---

(2002) (stating that rational basis is "a very difficult standard to meet" for those presenting substantive due process challenges).

42. The creation of affordable housing is a legitimate governmental purpose. See "Local Government Authority to Enact Inclusionary Zoning in North Carolina," below. *See also* Penn Central Transp. Co. v. New York City, 438 U.S. 104, 124–25 (1978) (stating that a local government is not precluded from passing zoning ordinances meant to address problems created in part by past zoning policies); Southern Burlington County N.A.A.C.P. v. Township of Mt. Laurel, 92 N.J. 158, 214, 456 A.2d 390, 418 (N.J. 1983); Home Builders Ass'n v. City of Napa, 90 Cal. App. 4th 188, 195 (2001).

43. Moore v. City of E. Cleveland, 431 U.S. 494, 498 (1977) (requiring "a rational relationship to permissible state objectives" (citing Euclid v. Ambler Realty Co., 272 U.S. 365 (1926))).

44. *See* Ferguson v. Skrupa, 372 U.S. 726, 730–32 (1963)(" We have returned to the original constitutional proposition that courts do not substitute their social and economic beliefs for the judgment of legislative bodies, who are elected to pass laws.").

45. *See* OWENS, note 30 above, at 217 n.4 ("It is the rare plaintiff who can prevail in a substantive due process challenge of a zoning restriction when this test is applied.").

46. Mathews v. Eldridge, 424 U.S. 319, 333 (1976) ("This Court consistently has held that some form of hearing is required before an individual is finally deprived of a property interest.").

47. *Id.* at 334 ("[D]ue process is flexible, and calls for such procedural protections as the particular situation demands." (quoting Morrissey v. Brewer, 408 U.S. 471, 481 (1972))). What process is due will depend on three factors: "[F]irst, the private interest that will be affected by the official action; second, the risk of an erroneous deprivation of such interest through the procedures used, and the probable value, if any, of additional or substitute procedural safeguards; and, finally, the Government's interest, including the function involved

established by a local government for other land use and zoning decisions should be adequate for purposes of an inclusionary zoning ordinance.[48]

Substantive Due Process in North Carolina

The North Carolina Constitution's "law of the land" clause[49] is synonymous with the Due Process Clause of the U.S. Constitution and thus presents similar protections and requirements.[50] North Carolina courts likewise grant substantial deference to local government legislative decisions. Land use practices such as inclusionary zoning will only be struck down if they are arbitrary and capricious, or if they fail to use reasonable means to address legitimate governmental objectives.[51]

Under the North Carolina Constitution, local government legislative decisions will not be ruled arbitrary and capricious as long as the government's action has a "reasonable tendency to promote the public good." [52] Such decisions are "entitled to implicit obedience."[53]

---

and the fiscal and administrative burdens that the additional or substitute procedural requirement would entail." *Id.* at 335.

48. For a more detailed discussion of the procedures due under both federal and North Carolina law, see OWENS, note 30 above, at 104.

49. N.C. CONST. art. I, § 19 ("No person shall be taken, imprisoned, or disseized of his freehold, liberties, or privileges, or outlawed, or exiled, or in any manner deprived of his life, liberty, or property, but by the law of the land. No person shall be denied the equal protection of the laws; nor shall any person be subjected to discrimination by the State because of race, color, religion, or national origin.").

50. *See* OWENS, note 30 above, at 217.

51. The requirement that governmental actions address legitimate objectives using reasonable means mirrors the takings test under North Carolina law. *See* A-S-P Associates v. City of Raleigh, 298 N.C. 207, 214, 258 S.E.2d 444, 448–49 (1979) ("First, is the object of the legislation within the scope of the police power? Second, considering all the surrounding circumstances and particular facts of the case is the means by which the governmental entity has chosen to regulate reasonable? This second inquiry is two-pronged: (1) Is the statute in its application reasonably necessary to promote the accomplishment of a public good and (2) is the interference with the owner's right to use his property as he deems appropriate reasonable in degree?") (citations omitted).

52. Marren v. Gamble, 237 N.C. 680, 686, 75 S.E.2d 880, 884 (1953).

53. *Id. See also* Zopfi v. City of Wilmington, 273 N.C. 430, 437, 160 S.E.2d 325, 332 (1968) (Courts "are not free to substitute their opinion for that of the legislative body so long as there is some plausible basis for the conclusion reached by that body.").

Procedural Due Process in North Carolina

In North Carolina, procedural due process applies to judicial and quasi-judicial procedures, such as requests for zoning variances, but not to the passage of legislation, so the enactment of an inclusionary zoning ordinance itself should not raise a procedural due process question.[54] Quasi-judicial processes, to the extent that they are incorporated as part of an inclusionary zoning ordinance, should include an evidentiary hearing [55] that provides the applicant with an opportunity to show that the particular project will not be feasible if the affordable housing requirement is imposed.[56]

Equal Protection

The right to "equal protection of the laws" is included in the Fourteenth Amendment of the U.S. Constitution.[57] This right means that a law that treats two individuals differently must be "reasonable, not arbitrary, and must rest upon some ground of difference having a fair and substantial relation to the object of the legislation."[58]

---

54. There is no requirement under North Carolina law for special notice of a legislative enactment. *See* Helms v. Charlotte, 255 N.C. 647, 652, 122 S.E.2d 817, 821 (1961); Capps v. City of Raleigh, 35 N.C. App. 290, 296–98, 241 S.E.2d 527, 530–32 (1978). *See also* County of Lancaster v. Mecklenburg County, 334 N.C. 496, 507, 434 S.E.2d 604, 612 (1993) (describing quasi-judicial decisions as efforts to "investigate facts, or ascertain the existence of facts, hold hearings, weigh evidence, and draw conclusions from them, as a basis for their official action, and to exercise discretion of a judicial nature").

55. *County of Lancaster*, 334 N.C. at 508, 434 S.E.2d at 612 (requiring "an evidentiary hearing with the right of the parties to offer evidence; cross-examine adverse witnesses; inspect documents; have sworn testimony; and have written findings of fact supported by competent, substantial, and material evidence" (citing Humble Oil & Ref. Co. v. Bd. of Aldermen I, 284 N.C. 458, 470, 202 S.E.2d 129, 137 (1974))).

56. The ordinance should also include plain, adequate, and complete remedies. *See* Johnston v. Gaston County, 71 N.C. App. 707, 712, 323 S.E.2d 381, 383 (1984) (citing Fair Assessment in Real Estate Ass'n v. McNary, 454 U.S. 100, 116 (1981)).

57. U.S. Const. amend. XIV, § 1 ("No State shall make or enforce any law which shall abridge the privileges or immunities of citizens of the United States; nor shall any State deprive any person of life, liberty, or property, without due process of law; nor deny to any person within its jurisdiction the equal protection of the laws."). In addition, the N.C. Constitution states, "No person shall be denied the equal protection of the laws." N.C. Const. art. 1, § 19.

58. Royster Guano Co. v. Virginia, 253 U.S. 412, 415 (1920).

Depending on the nature of the law being challenged, courts evaluate an equal protection claim using one of two standards of review: rational basis or strict scrutiny.[59]

If the law either involves a "suspect classification," such as race, or restricts certain "fundamental interests,"[60] a court will take the strict scrutiny approach. Note that a law that does not expressly involve a suspect classification might still be subjected to strict scrutiny if it is found to have a disparate impact and is intended to operate on the basis of the suspect classification.[61] Strict scrutiny requires the government to demonstrate that the challenged law furthers a compelling governmental interest and is narrowly drawn to do so.[62]

However, inclusionary zoning ordinances do not typically involve either suspect classifications or fundamental interests, and thus they are much more likely to be analyzed under the rational basis standard. Furthermore, courts give wide latitude to economic legislation,[63] and courts in other states have

---

59. The tests for determining the validity of an equal protection claim under North Carolina law parallel those under the U.S. Constitution. *See* OWENS, note 30 above, at 225 (citing Transylvania County v. Moody, 151 N.C.App. 389, 397, 565 S.E.2d 720, 726 (2002); Town of Atlantic Beach v. Young, 307 N.C. 422, 429, 298 S.E.2d 686, 691 (1983); and Texfi Indus., Inc. v. City of Fayetteville, 301 N.C. 1, 10, 269 S.E.2d 142, 149 (1980)).

60. As with substantive due process, fundamental interests are those that a court has found to be constitutionally significant (such as freedom of speech), and in the equal protection context, this generally means that the interest must be one protected by the U.S. Constitution. *See* San Antonio Indep. Sch. Dist. v. Rodriguez, 411 U.S. 1, 33 (1973) ("[T]he key to discovering whether [an interest] is 'fundamental' is not to be found in comparisons of . . . relative societal significance . . . . Nor is it to be found by weighing whether [one] is as important as [another]. Rather, the answer lies in assessing whether there is a right . . . explicitly or implicitly guaranteed by the Constitution.").

61. *See* Yick Wo v. Hopkins, 118 U.S. 356, 373–74 (1886) ("Though the law itself be fair on its face, and impartial in appearance, yet, if it is applied and administered by public authority with an evil eye and an unequal hand, so as practically to make unjust and illegal discriminations between persons in similar circumstances, material to their rights, the denial of equal justice is still within the prohibition of the constitution.").

62. *See* Memorial Hosp. v. Maricopa County, 415 U.S. 250, 254 (1974); White v. Pate, 308 N.C. 759, 766, 304 S.E.2d 199, 204 (1983).

63. *See* Cleburne v. Cleburne Living Ctr., Inc., 473 U.S. 432, 440 (1985). *See also* United States R.R. Retirement Bd. v. Fritz, 449 U.S. 166, 175 (1980) ("[T]he Court in cases involving social and economic benefits has consistently refused to invalidate on equal protection grounds legislation which it simply deemed unwise or unartfully drawn.").

shown reluctance to apply strict scrutiny to land use decisions.[64] The rational basis standard requires only that the law serve a legitimate government purpose and that any distinction it makes between groups be justified.[65] Thus, assuming an ordinance has a legitimate government purpose—which a local government would need to establish for both due process and statutory authority challenges—the analysis revolves around whether there is a sound basis for any distinction that the law makes.[66]

In order to succeed on an equal protection claim when the court is applying rational basis scrutiny, a challenger to an inclusionary zoning ordinance would have to show that there was no rational basis for any differential treatment of land within the local government's jurisdiction. This has occurred in North Carolina case law. For example, if a local ordinance subjects similarly situated persons engaged in the same business to different restrictions or privileges under the same conditions, the ordinance may be invalidated.[67]

Part 2: State Law Issues—Authority and Rent Control

Issues of constitutional law arise in all states and are generally uniform, with some minor exceptions depending on individual state constitutions. More variation is seen, however, with respect to two issues: local government

---

64. *See, e.g.*, Assoc. Home Builders, Inc. v. Livermore, 18 Cal. 3d 582, 603 (1976) ("To insist that such zoning laws are invalid unless the interests supporting the exclusion are compelling in character, and cannot be achieved by an alternative method, would result in wholesale invalidation of land use controls and endanger the validity of city and regional planning.").

65. *See* City of New Orleans v. Dukes, 427 U.S. 297, 303 (1976) ("When local economic regulation is challenged solely as violating the Equal Protection Clause, this Court consistently defers to legislative determinations as to the desirability of particular statutory discriminations. Unless a classification trammels fundamental personal rights or is drawn upon inherently suspect distinctions such as race, religion, or alienage, our decisions presume the constitutionality of the statutory discriminations and require only that the classification challenged be rationally related to a legitimate state interest." (citation omitted)).

66. Moore v. City of East Cleveland, 431 U.S. 494 (1977).

67. Suddreth v. City of Charlotte, 223 N.C. 630, 633, 27 S.E.2d 650, 653 (1943) ("Municipalities may classify persons according to their business and may apply different rules to different classes without violating constitutional rights, either under the State or Federal Constitution. The discriminations which invalidate an ordinance are those where persons engaged in the same business are subjected to different restrictions or are held entitled to different privileges under the same conditions.").

authority to enact inclusionary zoning and rent control laws. This section examines how these two issues may affect the legal status of inclusionary zoning in North Carolina.

Local Government Authority to Enact Inclusionary Zoning in North Carolina

As a threshold matter, a local government must first possess the legal authority to enact an inclusionary zoning ordinance. If a local government lacks such authority, the ordinance can be challenged as being *ultra vires*, meaning it exceeds the scope of the powers delegated to the local government.[68] In North Carolina, some inclusionary zoning programs have been in place for more than a decade, but none has been challenged in court. This section examines the rationale for such authority under current law and considers how a North Carolina court might evaluate an *ultra vires* challenge.

The source and extent of local government authority varies from state to state. Most states grant "home rule" to local governments, an authority that allows them to act on nearly all matters of local concern, with the exception of subject areas over which the state legislature has exclusive control.[69] North Carolina, however, is not a home rule state. North Carolina local governments are creatures of legislative benevolence, not constitutional mandate.[70] Accordingly, North Carolina local governments may only exert powers that are either expressly granted or permissibly implied from statutory grants of authority.

In North Carolina, an examination of local government authority involves three questions:

---

68. *See* Board of Supervisors v. De Groff Enters., 198 S.E.2d 600 (Va. 1973), superseded by statute, VA. CODE ANN. §§ 15.2-735.1, 15.2-2304, 15.2-2305 (invalidating an inclusionary zoning ordinance in part on the basis that it was *ultra vires*). *But cf.* Southern Burlington N.A.A.C.P. v. Mount Laurel Township (Mt. Laurel I), 336 A.2d 713 (N.J. 1983) (finding exclusionary zoning practices unconstitutional under state law); Southern Burlington N.A.A.C.P. v. Mount Laurel Township (Mt. Laurel II), 456 A.2d 390 (N.J. 1983) (directing municipalities to affirmatively provide an appropriate variety of affordable housing and offering mandatory set-aside programs as an acceptable means).

69. For more on the concept of home rule authority, see Frayda S. Bluestein, *Do North Carolina Local Governments Need Home Rule?* 84 N.C. L. REV. 1983, 1989–90 (2006).

70. A. Fleming Bell, Article 4, *The Police Power, in* COUNTY AND MUNICIPAL GOVERNMENT IN NORTH CAROLINA 2 (UNC School of Government 2007), *available at* www.sog.unc.edu/pubs/cmg/cmg04.pdf.

1. Is there an express prohibition of the activity?
2. Is there an express grant of authority for the activity?
3. In the absence of an express grant of authority, can authority be implied from existing grants of authority?

Each of these is applied to inclusionary zoning below.

No Express Prohibition of Inclusionary Zoning

North Carolina law does not expressly prohibit inclusionary zoning. On the contrary, the North Carolina General Assembly has expressly recognized, as a matter of public policy, the need for local governments to increase the supply of affordable residential housing for persons with lower incomes.[71] The state legislature has specifically addressed this need in one way, for example, by providing sweeping powers to public housing authorities and the Housing Finance Agency.[72] In neither case did the legislature limit the means of producing low-income housing to those means specifically enumerated by statute,[73] nor did it attempt to preempt or exclude local regulation in this area.

Express Authority for Inclusionary Zoning in North Carolina

Although no general prohibition exists in North Carolina, there is also no express grant of authority that is generally applicable to all local governments. However, the General Assembly has enacted a handful of local acts, applicable only to specific jurisdictions, containing express grants of authority to implement density bonus incentives that resemble voluntary inclusionary zoning.[74]

---

71. *See* G.S 157-2.

72. G.S. 157-9 (housing authorities for cities), 157-34 (housing authorities for counties). Cities and counties may themselves directly exercise powers granted by law to housing authorities. *See* G.S. 160A-456(b) (cities), 153A-376(b) (counties); G.S. Ch. 122A (North Carolina Housing Finance Agency).

73. Arguably the legislature did just the opposite in G.S. 157-9 when it established housing authorities "having all the powers necessary or convenient to carry out and effectuate the purposes and provisions of this Article . . ." and in G.S. 122A-5 when it established the Housing Finance Agency with "all of the powers necessary or convenient to carry out and effectuate the purposes and provisions of this Chapter, including, but without limiting the generality of the foregoing, the [following]. . . ."

74. *See, e.g.*, An Act Amending the Charter of the City of Wilmington to Authorize Zoning Density Bonuses in Projects Containing Specified Amounts of Low and Moderate Income Housing, 1991 N.C. Sess. Laws ch. 119; An Act Concerning Zoning by the City of Winston-Salem and Forsyth County, 1993 N.C. Sess. Laws ch. 588; An Act to Make

In each case, the legislature has either amended the local government's charter[75] or amended the application of the zoning-enabling statutes in relation to the local government.[76] Other local governments have attempted, but failed, to obtain similar local authority.[77] That local governments have sought such special authorization does not necessarily mean that they were required to do so. Arguably, the authority to enact some form of inclusionary zoning already exists, as discussed below. Local governments that have sought special authorization have chosen to avoid any ambiguity by obtaining legislation that addresses their programs directly.

Implied Authority of Local Governments to Enact Inclusionary Zoning

In the absence of an express prohibition or an express grant of authority, North Carolina law permits local government authority to be implied from other grants of power. In Sections 153A-4 and 160A-4 of the North Carolina General Statutes (hereinafter G.S.), the General Assembly calls for grants of authority to local governments to be broadly construed to include "any additional and supplementary powers that are reasonably necessary or expedient" to carry them into effect.[78] There are some instances, however, in which courts have taken a narrower view.

In *Homebuilders Association of Charlotte, Inc. v. City of Charlotte,* the North Carolina Supreme Court broadly construed the city's authority in upholding the imposition of user fees for a variety of city services—including special use permits, plat reviews, and building inspections—even though the

---

Various Amendments to Laws Applicable to Orange and Chatham Counties, 1991 N.C. Sess. Laws ch. 246.

75. *See* 1991 N.C. Sess. Laws ch. 119 (amending charter of the City of Wilmington); 1993 N.C. Sess. Laws ch. 588 (amending charter of City of Winston-Salem).

76. *See* 1991 N.C. Sess. Laws ch. 246, sec. 2 (amending application of G.S. 153A-340 to Orange County).

77. In both the 2001–2 and 2003–4 sessions of the North Carolina General Assembly, bills were introduced on behalf of communities in the Research Triangle region of the state seeking authority to enact mandatory inclusionary zoning ordinances. S 1001 (2001); S 493 (2003). Neither of the bills survived their respective legislative committee assignments. Such action could indicate opposition to granting the authority, or it might simply mean that the legislature believed at the time that such authority already existed.

78. G.S. 153A-4 and 160A-4.

city had no express statutory authority to impose them.[79] The court observed that the city held "express authority" to conduct the regulatory activities for which it was charging fees,[80] relying on the broad interpretation called for by G.S 160-4 to find implied authority for the fees.[81] The court was not persuaded by arguments that the legislature had already designated other means for paying the costs of development review (namely, property taxes) nor by arguments that the legislature had authorized the charging of fees for other activities but not for those being challenged. Instead, the court focused on the fact that the fees were reasonable and the authorizing legislation contained no prohibition against charging the fees.[82]

However, where the legislature clearly and unambiguously limits the means available to a local government for implementing an authority, other means of implementing the authority are not implied. For example, in *Smith Chapel Baptist Church v. City of Durham II*, the North Carolina Supreme Court rejected a city's attempt to charge a fee for management of a *comprehensive* stormwater program when the city's express statutory authority was "clearly and unambiguously" limited to charging fees only for the

---

79. 336 N.C. 37, 42, 442 S.E.2d 45, 49 (1994). ("The generally accepted rule today seems to be that the municipal power to regulate an activity implies the power to impose a fee in an amount sufficient to cover the cost of regulation."). *See also* OWENS, note 30 above, at 18–19.

80. *Homebuilders*, 336 N.C. at 43, 442 S.E.2d at 49 ("Thus, in this case, the services for which user fees are charged are all related to some express authority of the City to regulate the development of land.").

81. *Id*. at 43, 442 S.E.2d at 50.

82. *Id*. at 45, 442 S.E.2d at 51 (". . . the Court of Appeals based its decision—in part—on the fact that the General Assembly has expressly provided a means by which to meet the costs of regulating development, i.e., levying of taxes. There is, however, no language in the statute which restricts the municipalities to this method and the imposition of these fees does not appear to be contrary to State or federal law or the public policy of this State. The City has chosen a reasonable alternative by requiring that those who desire a particular service bear some of the costs associated with the provision of that service. Similarly, the Court of Appeals noted that the General Assembly has expressly authorized county water and sewer districts to charge user fees for furnished services while it has remained silent on the authority to impose user fees for other services. Here again, the General Assembly did not specify that sewer services were the only services for which user fees could be charged and we find no basis for such a strained reading of this statute.") (citations omitted).

management of the *physical systems*.[83] The court did not apply the statutory rule of broad construction in this case, because the plain meaning of the statute was clear and therefore required no judicial interpretation, whether strict or broad.[84]

The North Carolina Court of Appeals has applied this plain meaning rule in several cases, determining that the rule of broad construction "remains idle" when the plain meaning of a statute is "without ambiguity."[85] In one decision by the North Carolina Court of Appeals, the court omitted any discussion of the statutory call for broad construction and applied a strict interpretation.[86]

These legal contortions are understandably the source of some confusion on the issue of local government authority, and they provide courts with many avenues for evaluating local ordinances. As a consequence, in the absence of a specific statutory grant of authority or case law specifically on point, it is

---

83. 350 N.C. 805, 811, 517 S.E.2d 874, 879 (1999).

84. *Id.*

85. BellSouth Telecomms., Inc. v. City of Laurinburg, 168 N.C. App. 75, 82–83, 606 S.E.2d 721, 726 (2005); Durham Land Owners Ass'n v. County of Durham, 177 N.C. App. 629, 634, 630 S.E.2d 200, 203, *discretionary review denied*, 360 N.C. 532, 633 S.E.2d 678 (2006). *See also* Bluestein, note 69 above, at 2012 ("North Carolina courts have not consistently heeded this legislative directive to construe broadly local-enabling legislation. Instead, courts have intermittently applied Dillon's rule and other limiting rules of construction.").

86. *See* Union Land Owners Ass'n v. County of Union, ___ N.C. App. ___, 689 S.E.2d 504, 507 (2009) (mentioning the plain meaning rule before proceeding with a strict interpretation of the interaction of enabling statutes). It is unclear exactly how *Union Land Owners* would be applied in the context of inclusionary zoning, because that case could be distinguished from inclusionary zoning in any of the following ways: (1) *Union Land Owners* explained that the impact fees imposed in that case for school construction were not permitted tools under the zoning statute, whereas inclusionary zoning employs an authorized zoning tool by regulating the use of buildings to ensure a mix of units; (2) courts may take a more expansive view of how zoning tools may be employed in the context of affordable housing, which is an acknowledged consideration in zoning decisions and receives special statutory protection, *see, e.g.,* N.C.S.L. 2009-533 (making it unlawful to base land use decisions on the presence of affordable housing, and at the same time explicitly making it lawful to base land use decisions on prevention of over-concentration of affordable housing); and (3) municipalities have not been given the sole responsibility for providing affordable housing in the way that such a mandate exists for schools, *see* Durham Land Owners Ass'n v. County of Durham, 177 N.C. App. 629, 630 S.E.2d 200, *discretionary review denied*, 360 N.C. 532, 633 S.E.2d 678 (2006).

difficult to predict with certainty how a court would rule on the issue of local government authority to establish specific facets of an inclusionary zoning program.

Nonetheless, there are several statutory grants of authority to regulate land use that arguably contain implied authority to enact inclusionary zoning. For example, local governments have the authority to implement zoning,[87] the ability to regulate the development of subdivisions,[88] and a general police power.[89] The authority to enact inclusionary zoning ordinances could be found in each of these expressly delegated powers, and considered together, they provide a reasonable basis for enacting a local program. Each is discussed briefly below.

Zoning power. North Carolina law expressly authorizes local governments, "for the purpose of promoting health, safety, morals and general welfare . . . [to] regulate and restrict the height, number of stories and size of buildings and other structures, the percentage of lots that may be occupied, the size of yards, courts and other open spaces, the *density of population*, and the *location and use of buildings, structures, and land*."[90] Zoning regulations "shall be designed to promote the public health, safety and general welfare," and by statute, the regulations may be drawn to serve an open-ended set of public purposes.[91] However, how a court would interpret this grant of authority in the context of inclusionary zoning is not entirely clear.

On its face, the zoning power appears to provide the necessary authority to implement inclusionary zoning. The intended purposes of the zoning power cover a broad range of activities; the General Assembly has called for broad interpretation of local government authority;[92] there is a long-standing rule of case law indicating that zoning regulations, as long as they are reasonable,

---

87. G.S. 153A-340 and 160A-381.

88. G.S. 153A-331 and 160A-372.

89. G.S. 153A-121 and 160A-174.

90. G.S. 153A-340, 160A-381 (emphasis added).

91. G.S. 153A-341; 160A-383 ("[T]he regulations may address, *among other things*, the following public purposes: to provide adequate light and air; to prevent the overcrowding of land; to avoid undue concentration of population; to lessen congestion in the streets; to secure safety from fire, panic, and dangers; and to facilitate the efficient and adequate provision of transportation, water, sewerage, schools, parks, *and other public requirements*.") (emphasis added).

92. G.S. 153A-4 and 160A-4.

are presumed to be valid in North Carolina;[93] and housing affordability has long been an assumed component of zoning, as evidenced by statutes that prohibit the exclusion of manufactured homes (for the explicitly stated purpose of providing affordable housing opportunities) and, most recently, by fair housing laws addressing land use decisions that consider the concentration of affordable housing.[94]

However, the North Carolina Court of Appeals has also articulated some limits to the zoning power—at least in the context of school impact fees—by declaring that a zoning ordinance must use "the tools authorized by the zoning statute."[95] The use of other tools, the court concluded, falls outside the local government's legislatively granted zoning powers.[96]

This suggests that the validity of an inclusionary zoning ordinance may turn on whether it properly employs the available tools in the zoning statute; namely, the authority to regulate and restrict "the location and use of build-

---

93. *See* Marren v. Gamble, 237 N.C. 680, 75 S.E.2d 880 (1953) (determining that since a delegation of the state's zoning power to a municipality "has a reasonable tendency to promote the public good, it represents a valid exercise of the police power, and is entitled to implicit obedience."); *In re* Parker, 214 N.C. 51, 55, 197 S.E. 706, 709 (1938) ("When the most that can be said against [zoning] ordinances is that whether it was an unreasonable, arbitrary or unequal exercise of power is fairly debatable, the courts will not interfere. In such circumstances the settled rule seems to be that the court will not substitute its judgment for that of the legislative body charged with the primary duty and responsibility of determining whether its action is in the interest of the public health, safety, morals or general welfare."). *See also* County of Lancaster v. Mecklenburg County, 334 N.C. 496, 510, 434 S.E.2d 604, 614 (1993) (citing Marren v. Gamble and *In re* Parker for the conclusion that "[a] zoning ordinance is presumed valid, and the courts will defer to the governing board's legislative judgment unless it is clearly unreasonable or an abuse of discretion"); OWENS, note 30 above, at 277.

94. North Carolina's fair housing statute, G.S. 41A-4, makes it unlawful to base land use decisions on the presence of affordable housing in a development, but it specifically exempts land use decisions based on limiting high concentrations of affordable housing, and one of the bases for enacting inclusionary zoning is to limit the concentration of affordable housing. See also "Creation of affordable housing as a legitimate public purpose in North Carolina," below.

95. *See* Union Land Owners Ass'n v. County of Union, ___ N.C. App. ___, ___, 689 S.E.2d 504, 507 (2009).

96. *Id.* It remains to be seen how this interpretation might be applied (if at all) in the inclusionary zoning context, because the decision was rendered without applying either the plain meaning rule (although the court cites the plain meaning rule, it does not appear to have applied this rule) or the statutory call for broad construction, and the school impact fee context provides occasion to distinguish the case from inclusionary zoning. *See also* note 86, above.

ings, structures, and land for trade, industry, residence and other purposes."[97] These tools should be adequate for most inclusionary zoning ordinances, which regulate location and use according to the affordability of residential units.

It is reasonable to conclude that affordability is a valid use category for two reasons. First, use categories are not further defined by statute and have never been restricted only to broad categories such as residential, commercial, or industrial. North Carolina zoning ordinances have for decades defined narrow categories of use that are not explicitly identified in the zoning statute.[98] Contemporary zoning ordinances may include dozens of use districts, and in the residential context alone, narrow categories of use are frequently employed—for example, single-family residences on large lots, single-family residences on small lots, duplexes, small apartment buildings, and high-rise residential buildings.[99] Other use categories have been upheld by the courts even when not mentioned in authorizing statutes; these include manufactured homes,[100] adult businesses,[101] and signs.[102] Second, as already mentioned above, affordability has been explicitly acknowledged by statute as a valid consideration in certain land use decisions.[103]

Subdivision power. Subdivision statutes generally address the creation of new lots by dividing larger plots of land. North Carolina grants local governments the power to "provide for the orderly growth and development" of their communities and to manage "the distribution of population . . . in a manner that will avoid congestion and overcrowding and will create conditions that substantially promote public health, safety and the general welfare."[104] Inclusionary zoning arguably addresses these concerns by ensuring that new growth does not exclude housing that is affordable to moderate- or

---

97. G.S. 153A-340; 160A-381.

98. *See* OWENS, note 30 above, at 34.

99. *Id.*

100. *See, e.g.*, City of Raleigh v. Morand, 247 N.C. 363, 100 S.E.2d 870 (1957) (upholding regulation of manufactured housing prior to the time that the General Assembly enacted specific statutory authority for regulating that narrow category of residential use).

101. *See, e.g.,* Onslow County v. Moore, 129 N.C. App. 376, 499 S.E.2d 780, *review denied*, 349 N.C. 361, 525 S.E.2d 453 (1998).

102. *See, e.g.*, Summey Outdoor Adver. Inc. v. County of Henderson, 96 N.C. App. 533, 538, 386 S.E.2d 439, 443 (1989), *review denied*, 326 N.C. 486, 392 S.E.2d 101 (1990).

103. See note 94, above.

104. G.S. 153A-331(a) (counties); 160A-372(a) (cities).

lower-income households. This, in turn, may prevent overcrowding in lower-income areas and distribute housing in an orderly fashion throughout the community.

Recall, however, that the North Carolina Court of Appeals has held that the means of achieving a public purpose are limited to those tools identified in authorizing statutes.[105] The means provided by the subdivision authority include setting standards for the size of lots, the layout of public facilities, and the provision of essential infrastructure.[106] When these tools are viewed in the inclusionary zoning context, the subdivision power permits a local government to require owners, at the time of subdivision, to establish lot sizes and infrastructure that will be conducive to the construction of affordable housing, whether single-family, multifamily, or mixed-use.[107]

Additionally, the subdivision power authorizes local governments to require developers to dedicate rights-of-way for streets, sites for schools, and fees for recreation. Dedications can also be required for the construction of community service facilities, such as daycare centers, police substations, and health facilities, which could be intentionally co-located or associated with affordable housing units.[108]

However, the subdivision power does not contain explicit authority for the dedication of sites or fees for affordable housing.[109] Such dedications, it must be pointed out, are not a necessary component of an inclusionary zoning ordinance and are rarely required. Most inclusionary zoning ordinances

---

105. *See* Union Land Owners Ass'n v. County of Union, ___ N.C. App. ___, 689 S.E.2d 504 (2009).

106. G.S. 153A-331 (counties); 160A-372 (cities).

107. *Id.*

108. G.S. 153A-331(c) (counties); 160A-372(c) (cities). The term "community service facilities" is not further defined in North Carolina statutes or case law, but as it is commonly understood in North Carolina and used in other states, the term includes common facilities such as water and sewer facilities, police and fire stations, social and recreational centers, hospitals, daycare centers, and other providers of social, health, and welfare services. *See, e.g.,* First Nat'l Bank of Lake Forest v. Lake County, 130 N.E.2d 267 (1955); Sunderland Family Treatment Servs. v. City of Pasco, 26 P.3d 955 (2001). *Cf.* I.R.C. § 42(d)(4)(C)(iii) (2006) (defining a community service facility in the context of the federal low-income housing tax credit as a facility designed to serve primarily individuals whose income is 60 percent or less of area median income).

109. G.S. 153A-331; 160A-372. *See* Owens, note 30 above, at 40, 49.

are designed to leave inclusionary units in private hands, not to have them dedicated over to the local government.[110]

Police power. The general police power gives broad authority to North Carolina local governments to "define, prohibit, regulate, or abate acts, omissions, or conditions, detrimental to the health, safety, or welfare of its citizens."[111] This delegation of authority grants local governments the power to regulate both activity and land use within their boundaries, even if the regulations result in "pecuniary injury" to a party.[112] While the courts had previously found that the police power provides a source of authority for land use regulations,[113] ordinances enacted under the police power that "substantially affect land use" must now comply with the requirements and limitations applicable to zoning ordinances.[114] It is not difficult to conclude that an inclusionary zoning ordinance substantially affects land use. Therefore, even if a local government intends to rely upon the general police power to enact an inclusionary zoning ordinance, the ordinance now must essentially

---

110. As a practical matter, however, some developers may ultimately prefer to sell inclusionary units to a nonprofit or government agency or to retain ownership but turn management over to some other agency. See "Managing Inclusionary Units" in Chapter 7.

111. G.S.153A-140; 160A-174.

112. "[T]he mere fact of pecuniary injury does not warrant the overthrow of legislation of a police character." Suddreth v. City of Charlotte, 223 N.C. 630, 634, 27 S.E.2d 650, 653–654 (1943).

113. *See, e.g.,* Summey Outdoor Adver. Inc. v. County of Henderson, 96 N.C. App. 533, 538, 386 S.E.2d 439, 443 (1989) ("We do not believe that because defendant has authority to regulate signs under G.S. 153A-340, it may not regulate signs in a similar manner under the general police powers in G.S. 153A-121. G.S. 153A-121 and 153A-340 do not operate exclusively of each other."). *See also* OWENS, note 30 above, at 18.

114. Two recent decisions highlight the change in direction taken by the North Carolina Court of Appeals. First, the court held that an ordinance that "substantially affects land use" must comply with the notice requirements set forth in the zoning statutes or it will be invalidated. Thrash Ltd. P'ship v. County of Buncombe, 195 N.C. App. 727, 673 S.E.2d 689 (2009). Second, the court stated—in the context of an adequate public facilities ordinance (APFO) imposing school impact fees—that the general police power does *not* provide an independent source of authority from the zoning or subdivision authority, directly contradicting *Summey.* Union Land Owners Ass'n v. County of Union, ___ N.C. App. ___, ___, 689 S.E.2d 504, 506 (2009) ("[The police power] does not provide an independent source of authority for the APFO. Any contrary decision would eviscerate existing limitations on defendant's zoning subdivision regulation authority.").

comply with the procedural requirements and limitations applicable to a zoning ordinance, or it risks being invalidated.

Creation of affordable housing as a legitimate public purpose in North Carolina. In North Carolina, local government interest in providing affordable housing is beyond question. Affordable housing has been recognized as a legitimate government purpose in state supreme court decisions[115] as well as in statutes.[116] For instance, the legislature provides local governments with the power to address affordable housing through the creation of housing authorities pursuant to the state's housing authority law.[117] As a justification for the law, the legislature stated that "it is in the best interest of the State to encourage programs to provide housing for . . . [low income] persons without imposing on them undue financial hardship; and that in undertaking such programs a housing authority is promoting the health, welfare and prosperity of all citizens of the State and is serving a public purpose for the benefit of the general public."[118] Local governments are not required to establish a housing authority in order to exercise the powers granted under the Housing Authorities Law. They may exercise that power directly and independently pursuant

---

115. Wells v. Hous. Auth. of Wilmington, 213 N.C. 744, 197 S.E.2d 693 (1938); Martin v. North Carolina Hous. Corp., 277 N.C. 29, 175 S.E.2d 665 (1970) (concluding that the North Carolina Housing Corporation, which was created by the General Assembly to provide low-income residential housing, was created for a public purpose).

116. *See, e.g.,* G.S. Ch. 157, Art. 1 (§§ 157-1 to 157-39.8).

117. *Id.*

118. G.S. 157-2(b). See also North Carolina's Urban Redevelopment statute, G.S. 160A-503(2) (defining "blighted area" as one "which, by reason of dilapidation, deterioration, age or obsolescence, inadequate provision for ventilation, light, air, sanitation, or open spaces, high density of population and overcrowding, unsanitary or unsafe conditions, or the existence of conditions which endanger life or property by fire and other causes, or any combination of such factors, substantially impairs the sound growth of the community, is conducive to ill health, transmission of disease, infant mortality, juvenile delinquency and crime, and is detrimental to the public health, safety, morals or welfare") and Community Development statutes, G.S. 160A-456 (authorizing, *inter alia*, "Programs of assistance and financing of rehabilitation of private buildings principally for the benefit of low and moderate income persons, or for the restoration or preservation of older neighborhoods or properties, including direct repair, the making of grants or loans, the subsidization of interest payments on loans, and the guaranty of loans," as well as the use of Community Development Block Grant funds), and G.S. 160A-457 (authorizing the acquisition of property that is blighted or appropriate for housing construction or rehabilitation).

to authority granted by G.S. 160A-456 (cities) and 153A-376 (counties). The Housing Authorities Law provides sweeping authority for the construction and management of affordable housing, and it clearly evinces a position of the General Assembly that is strongly in favor of the provision of affordable housing as a valid public purpose. It does not, however, grant explicit authority to enact inclusionary zoning.

North Carolina Limitation on Rent Control

Section 42-14.1 of the North Carolina General Statutes provides that "No county or city . . . may enact . . . any ordinance or resolution which regulates the amount of rent to be charged for privately owned, single-family or multiple unit residential or commercial rental property." However, exceptions are allowed for "(1) Regulating in any way property belonging to that city, county, or authority; (2) Entering into agreements with private persons which regulate the amount of rent charged for subsidized rental properties; or (3) Enacting ordinances or resolutions restricting rent for properties assisted with Community Development Block Grant Funds."

If applied in the context of inclusionary zoning, rent restrictions on inclusionary set-aside housing appear to be in jeopardy under the statute. However, if the developer conveys units to the local government or a public agency or enters into an agreement on the control of rents, the inclusionary zoning program would fall into one of the exceptions.

Some advocates argue that inclusionary zoning ordinances are distinct from traditional rent control,[119] and thus a rent control ban like North Carolina's has no application to inclusionary zoning ordinances. There are four arguments for distinguishing inclusionary zoning from traditional rent control. First, it has been argued that inclusionary zoning is a remedial response to the effects of exclusionary zoning, not a form of rent control. Second, advocates point out that inclusionary zoning applies primarily to new developments and not to existing dwellings, whereas traditional rent control typically applies to all rental dwellings. Third, both rental and home-ownership programs can be included in an inclusionary zoning ordinance,

---

119. *See, e.g.*, Nadia I. El Mallakh, Comment, *Does the Costra-Hawkins Act Prohibit Local Inclusionary Zoning Programs*, 89 Cal. L. Rev. 1847, 1862 (2001) ("[I]nclusionary zoning is a unique, necessary land use tool that should not be confused with rent control.").

but traditional rent control applies only to rental properties.[120] Finally, unlike most traditional rent control programs, which apply to any renter regardless of means, inclusionary zoning typically includes screening processes for tenants and is designed specifically to benefit lower-income households.[121]

However, the basic concept of rent control, under which landowners retain ownership of their property but restrictions are placed on the economic return that may be realized from the property, arguably applies in the inclusionary zoning context as well. Additionally, courts in Colorado and Wisconsin have determined that inclusionary zoning programs are subject to those states' respective rent control statutes.[122] It is possible to distinguish those out-of-state cases from application in North Carolina, and the cases are not binding on North Carolina courts in any event.[123] Nevertheless, it remains possible that a North Carolina inclusionary zoning program could fall under the purview of the state's rent control statute.

If the North Carolina rent control statute were found to be applicable, inclusionary affordable units would arguably fall within the enumerated exception for subsidized rental housing for which the amount of rent charged is regulated by an agreement between the local government and the property owner.

To qualify under this exception, a rental property must meet two basic requirements. First, the property must be subsidized. Most inclusionary zon-

---

120. Barbara Ehrlich Kautz, *In Defense of Inclusionary Zoning: Successfully Creating Affordable Housing*, 36 U.S.F. L. Rev. 971, 1011 (2002).

121. *See* Mallakh, note 119 above, at 1875.

122. Town of Telluride v. Lot Thirty-Four Venture, L.L.C., 3 P.3d 30, 35 (Colo. 2000) (determining that state rent control statute, Colo. Rev. Stat. § 38-12-301, superseded town's authority; that inclusionary zoning ordinance not intended as exception to the statute; and that inclusionary zoning ordinance "operated to suppress rental values below their market values."); Apt. Ass'n of S. Cent. Wisconsin, Inc. v. City of Madison, 722 N.W.2d 614, 622 (Wis. Ct. App. 2006) (finding that city's mandatory inclusionary zoning ordinance violated state ban on municipal rent control, and ordinance itself could not serve as "an agreement with a private person who regulates rent or fees" and thereby fall into an exception to the statute).

123. For instance, the Colorado statute discussed in *Lot Thirty-Four,* above, only provides an exception for property in which a state or local government body has an interest. North Carolina, on the other hand, has a much broader set of exemptions that include city-, county- or housing authority-owned property, subsidized properties where there is an agreement with a third party as to rent, and properties assisted with Community Development Block Grants.

ing programs contain some form of subsidy, such as a density bonus, fast-track permitting services, or other incentive provided as part of the inclusionary zoning program.[124] Second, an agreement must be reached between the owner and the local government. Agreements regarding development[125] or management[126] of affordable housing under an inclusionary zoning program fulfill the second requirement.[127]

---

124. The term "subsidized" is not further defined in the statute, so there appears to be no minimum amount of subsidy or form of subsidy required for a rental property to fall under the exception of G.S. 42-14.1(2). Affordable housing is frequently subsidized with relatively small local government grants, by provision of mortgage insurance benefiting a lender, or through tax-credit programs such as the federal Low Income Housing Tax Credit program. Therefore, a reasonable interpretation of "subsidized" would include incentives such as density bonuses, fee waivers, and even expedited permit processing (fast-track permitting) if developers would ordinarily be required to pay a fee for such expedited service.

125. See "Development Plans and Agreements" in Chapter 6.

126. See "Managing Inclusionary Units" in Chapter 7.

127. A Wisconsin appellate court, in *Apartment Association of South Central Wisconsin, Inc. v. City of Madison*, 722 N.W.2d 614 (Wis. Ct. App. 2006), ruled that an arguably similar exception to that state's rent control statute did not apply when the city claimed that *the ordinance itself* was an agreement between the municipality and the landowner. The court ruled that the ordinance itself could not constitute an agreement, emphasizing the mandatory nature of the ordinance. This case suggests that local governments would be wise to enter into *separate* agreements of some kind for the provision and management of affordable set-aside units.

Index

D

Dare County, N.C.
    level of compulsion, 30–31
    preferential residency status, 107
    unit prices, setting, 47

Davidson, N.C.
    covered developments, 37–38
    integration of units into development, 84–86
    land donation, 74
    level of compulsion, 29
    in-lieu payments, 71–72
    management of inclusionary units, 98–99
    qualification of eligible residents, 101
    set-aside percentage of affordable units, 39–40, 41–42
    tenancy or manner of ownership consistency, 89

dedications of property required as condition of land use approval. *See* takings

deed restrictions, deeds of trust, and ground leases, 110–12

density bonuses, 56–58
    defined, 13n5, 56
    effectiveness of plans with, 8, 10, 12n4
    in housing needs assessments, 15n32
    in voluntary programs, 29, 30

Department of Housing and Urban Development, U.S. (HUD)
    HUD consolidated plan, 14n28
    qualifying household income level, setting, 43

developable land, availability of, 10

developer compliance. *See* compliance issues

development plans and agreements with local governments, 89–92, 153

development standards, relaxation of, 60–62

Dolan v. City of Tigard, 51n16, 77n1, 78nn12–13, 127n5, 130–31n23, 131n25

donations of land, 74–77

due process, 133–37

durational residency preferences, 105, 107–8, 122–23nn5–6

Durham Land Owners Ass'n v. County of Durham, 79n18, 144nn85–86

E

economic infeasibility claims, 128n11

eligible residents, qualification of, 98, 100–104

energy efficiency requirements, 83

environmental requirements, 93

equal protection under the law, 105, 137–39

equity sharing, 116–19

Euclid v. Ambler Realty Co., 129n14, 134n41, 135n43

exactions, 69, 130–31, 133